The **Fiona Harrold** Coaching Series

More
Than Money

Gráinne O'Malley

7 Steps to wealth
and prosperity

HODDER
MOBIUS

First published in Great Britain in 2005 by Hodder and Stoughton
A division of Hodder Headline

The right of Gráinne O'Malley to be identified as the Author
of the Work has been asserted by her in accordance with the
Copyright, Designs and Patents Act 1988

A Mobius Book

1

A CIP catalogue record for this title is
available from the British Library

ISBN 0 340 83706 3

Typeset in Stone Serif by Palimpsest Book Production Limited,
Polmont, Stirlingshire
Printed and bound by Clays Ltd, St Ives plc

Hodder Headline's policy is to use papers that are natural,
renewable and recyclable products and made from wood grown in
sustainable forests. The logging and manufacturing processes are
expected to conform to the environmental regulations of the country
of origin

Hodder and Stoughton Ltd
A division of Hodder Headline
338 Euston Road
London NW1 3BH

Contents

Contents

Acknowledgements

For Kevin, the other half of everything.

A heartfelt thank you to Hodder and Stoughton who so patiently accommodated my writing of this book. Helen Coyle, your gentle urging brought it home. Thank you to Sheila Crowley at AP Watt, for believing in the idea and to the inimitable Fiona Harrold for having it. You change the world, Fiona. Thank you to Mrs Carty who, by inspiring me to read, inspired me to write and to all the other amazing women who have enriched my life and continue to do so. You know who you are. Finally, my deepest thanks to all of you who trusted me with your money stories. Know that your courage has eased the way for those who follow. I honour you.

Foreword from Fiona Harrold

Gráinne O'Malley is the smartest person I know on money. As soon as I met her nearly five years ago and heard her talk, I knew she was the Wealth Coach I had been waiting for and she immediately joined my team. Since then, she has helped many individuals transform their relationship with money and achieve sound financial health – and wealth. She instinctively understands the psychology around this in a way I've never heard before. She's made money, lost it and made it again and even married an accountant! She's studied people with it and people without it; she's studied people's attitudes to it, and has read every book ever written on the subject. Her conclusion? Money is one thorny subject for many of us. We're less comfortable disclosing what we earn than the last time we had sex!

Do you spend more than you earn? Do you find shopping compulsive? Does money or the lack of it shape your life and your happiness? Are you in debt and would rather not be? If you want to make money your friend, let Gráinne introduce you! Seriously. If you want to get a handle on money and control your finances once and for all, *More Than Money* will show you how to. This is one investment I guarantee will pay dividends.

Gráinne is passionate about money and teaching us all how to take control of this fundamental part of our lives. Apply her simple, proven strategies and change your relationship to money forever – and let us know how you get on. You'll find us at www.fionaharrold.com

Good luck!

Fiona Harrold
London, 2005

1

Know Yourself

The highest use of capital is not to make more money, but to make money do more for the betterment of life

HENRY FORD

I love money! So tie me up and burn me at the stake for such blasphemy. Isn't money the root of all evil, filthy lucre, the road to ruin, just plain dirty? Well, I've lived with it and I've lived without it and I can tell you that all the things that 'money doesn't buy' are a whole lot easier to enjoy when you have money. It is much more pleasant to take a walk in the park or stop to smell the roses when there is money in the bank to pay the mortgage. Funny then, that just having pots of money doesn't guarantee a life enjoying those things it can and can't buy. And that there are people who enjoy life thoroughly on very little money.

It's not just about more money; it's clearly about more than money.

Let me tell you another little-known thing about money: money is fun. It hangs around with people who know how to enjoy it, who know how to show it a good time. It loves to move from person to person, to be exchanged for something great and move on to the next exciting adventure. It does not like to be restricted. It does not spend time with people who are afraid of it or don't like it. It spends time with generous people. It spends time with people who value it.

Doesn't that sound like a great place to be with money? Just for a moment imagine your life without money concerns. More than that, imagine what it would be like to spend more time planning for fun things in your life, or thinking about what you really want to achieve, than about how you are going to pay the bills. If that is a little difficult for you at the moment, take heart. Wherever you are with money right now, you're headed somewhere fabulous and I am delighted to be stepping out with you on this journey. By the end of this book you are going to know what it feels like not to have to worry about money. You are going to know what it feels like to be in command of your finances. You are going to know what it feels like to wake up in the morning and be free to focus all your energy on loving life.

UNDERSTANDING YOUR MONEY CAN BE EASY AND FUN

I know that you are the kind of person who demands much from life. The fact that you are reading this tells me that you are the kind of person who will search for the answers you need to get you to where you want to go. And right now you are ready to address money. Welcome aboard, you are in the right place. I am so excited for you. I am excited because I know what happens to a life that is freed of financial constraints. It blossoms, it glows, it explodes with freshness and boundless energy. It can be lived in pursuit of your greatness. After years of being restricted from being all it can be, life finally gets to live. This is possible for everyone. I know this because I have seen it over and over again. The problem is not that there is some complex financial secret that only a few can understand. The problem is in fact that there are a few simple financial rules and truths that have not been part of our basic education. Regardless of where you are starting from, once you have these tools you will be amazed at how easy it is to understand, manage and master your money.

MY STORY

I always hated accounts. Maths was my worst subject at school, and accounting was my worst subject in management training. I could never be sure that my two and two would equal four with or without a calculator. I was afraid of numbers. When I got out in the real world however (my first career was in hotel management), I found that when numbers reflected actual events and circumstances they were easier to understand. More than that, they were fascinating. When I looked at a statement of profit and loss, I saw couples sitting down in the restaurant ordering dinner and the cook in the kitchen walking to the store to get ingredients that were delivered from the supplier with whom I had talked the day before. The accounts told me a story; a story about people whose lives I was interested in. The profit line told me that we would be able to employ the young man we had interviewed for a summer job and he in turn would be able to save for his first college fees. It told me that my boss would get her bonus and she would build the extension that she wanted on her house. When you followed the story, accounts were easy to understand. I have always since wondered why couldn't we have learned that in accounts class? Why do accounts, finance and money have to appear so complicated?

Everyone deserves a second chance

In 1997, as part of a course I was interested in, I found myself attending a seminar module on money. The module was actually about how to invest in the stock market, something I had never even considered doing. I sat in the room with 200 other people, many of whom were successful businessmen and women and I felt totally out of my league. But the course was fun and I enjoyed myself, so much so I didn't notice I was learning anything. By the end of the weekend, I was hooked. I was hooked on how easy it was to understand money, how easy it was to trade on the stock market, how easy it was to make complex calculations, how easy it was to love numbers when someone explains them to you clearly.

> A little financial knowledge goes a long way

For the next two years, I studied everything I could get my hands on about money and the stock market. I quit my job, traded stocks on-line and I hung out with people who did the same. I made money, I lost money, and I made money, over and over again. It was the heady days of the dot com boom when stock prices doubled and halved in hours, sometimes in minutes. It was an exhilarating, live financial roller-coaster ride. Somewhere along the way, the making or losing became secondary. I became fascinated with what I was learning about money and people's attitudes to it. I learned more about the relationship between money, mind and emotion during those two years than I did in all the years before or since.

MONEY AND EMOTION

I watched as friends traded the same stock, planning the same play, and while one would make money the other would lose money. How could that be? Even more bizarre, I saw people make huge amounts of money, lose it all and be glad of it. I saw people risk the pounds they had already made, trying to make another few pennies and others who took pennies when there were pounds to be taken. Finally, I saw myself turn off my trading account one day and not turn it on again for eighteen months. I was sick of the roller-coaster. No matter how much money there was to be made, I was numb. But I'd learned the biggest lesson of all: I'd learned that, drained of emotion, money is nothing. It has no power except the power we give it. And what we give it determines what it gives back to us.

Unfortunately, in our society, the emotion most people attach to money is fear. There is the fear of not being able to meet the bills, the fear of not being able to provide for the kids, the fear of having to work so hard life will pass you by, the fear of not being able to afford the clothes to look good enough or not being able to buy the right house, the fear of being out of control, the fear of not being able to provide for retirement, the fear of losing what we have, the fear of being vulnerable, fear for our very survival. So many, many financial fears consuming our minds, making our bodies tired, our minds weary, our relationships strained and our lives overwhelmed.

DON'T FEEL THE FEAR ANY MORE

The biggest goal on the road to wealth and prosperity is to get above the fear. It's also the easiest goal to achieve. It's actually that simple. We're not going to study rocket science here and it's not going to take years of practice to perfect. By the time you finish this book, and finish it you will, you will have tools that will allow you not to worry about money ever again. Any time you have a money concern, a solution will pop into your head. You will never be able to un-know what you will know. It's simply a question of information. Fear is deceptive. Remember Dorothy in *The Wizard of Oz*. When she finally found the wizard she was very afraid. The thunderous voice, the enormous presence, the unfamiliar environment, all conspired to make her feel small, unworthy and incapable – until Toto pulled aside the curtain and revealed a little old man more frightened than frightening. Once the mystery was uncovered and the wizard's power diminished, Dorothy found that she had all the answers within herself.

The same is true of money management. Much of what appears daunting is just smokescreen and loudspeakers, jargon and double-entry double-speak. So the first thing we are going to do is pull back the curtain and look the wizard in the eye. We're going to do this from two angles. At the end of each chapter I will be setting you tasks divided into two elements. First, you will have a task or tasks designed to help you identify and understand your own personal financial psychology. These tasks will help you to find out why you do what you do financially. Second, you will have tasks that are simple numbers exercises. These are designed, step by step, to build up a real, accounts-based, blueprint for your life. You will be amazed at how simple it is to build a comprehensive financial representation of your life.

HOW TO USE THIS BOOK

I know that you are the kind of person who wants quick results. I am too. So I have designed these exercises to get those results by the shortest, fastest route. Who wants to spend hours and hours poring over financial data or contemplating your financial navel? Not you, I know. You want to get the information, apply it and move on. All you have to do is work the process, step by step, until you get to the end. Skip nothing, apply yourself with your usual fervour, dedication and commitment and you will triumph. I commit to 100 per cent focus on you in each and every chapter and I expect the same from you. I will be straight with you, I won't waste your time. I am not here to give you financial advice. I am not going to give you any answers. I am going to give you some information and ask lots of questions. There may be times when you will be uncomfortable with the questions I will ask you. There may be times when you just don't want to know what the numbers add up to, or don't add up to. But let me ask you this. Is a few moments of discomfort a high price to pay for a lifetime of financial peace of mind? I thought not! Let's get to work.

> To understand your money, you must first understand yourself

Work, did I say work? Silly me, I must have been thinking of some other book. I mean, of course, let's have some fun. Have you ever found yourself sitting in a café, sipping coffee and watching the world go by? You know, the kind of moment when you dally through an hour watching people, trying to guess why they are doing the things they are doing and not even noticing time go past. My favourite place to do this is on the pavement cafés of the Champs-Elysées in Paris. There is nowhere else I have found where quite so much of the world passes one spot in one hour. You find everyone from the most elegant of society ladies, to students, to artists, to business people, to simply ordinary people from hundreds of cultures and countries, all with a myriad of reasons for being there, expressing a profusion of behaviours: giveaway clues to their characters and lives. I usually have a glass of freshly squeezed orange juice or a steaming hot chocolate (depending on the season), with a flaky butter croissant while I ponder the lives of those who pass, wondering where they grew up, what kind of family they might have had or currently have, why they pick those shoes with that dress, or choose that book to read, or sit with those people. It's a dreamy process this examining the lives of others.

That's exactly how I want you to approach the exercises in this first chapter. I want you to sit down in a café, sip a coffee, and allow yourself to wonder why you do the things you do and where you may have learned to make those choices. It can be that easy. Why is it that we will voluntarily dissect the behaviours of others with relish, but when we come to examining our own behaviours, it suddenly seems such a threatening thing? If it worked better the hard way, I'd be all for it. But it doesn't. It is much more productive to examine ourselves without the drama, without the anguish, without the guilt, shame, resentment, frustration, and so on that we are all too keen to heap on ourselves but would never entertain when examining a friend. We are much kinder to our friends than we are to ourselves. But that stops here! From here on, you will treat yourself with the same respect and kindness that you would your best friend going through a sticky patch.

YOUR MONEY IS YOUR BUSINESS

Speaking of best friends, let me briefly mention those people close to you who may be affected by your decision to take full and personal responsibility for your money. If you are currently in a situation where you share financial responsibility and decision-making, you may want to consider how you will best communicate your new financial awareness to those involved. Be warned. This does not mean assuming the right to tell others how things ought to be done from now on. Just as I do not assume to know what is right for you, you must not assume to know what is right for them. This is a one-seat booking. The only person who committed to the trip is you. They may or may not support you, they may or may not know that you are reading this book or tackling this subject. You may or may not want even to tell them. Whatever the circumstances, the only person you are taking charge of is you and whether you choose to share the information (in a kind and understanding manner), or not, is up to you.

That said, there are a few things you can do to make your transition as pleasant as possible for others. The very first thing you are going to write down in the beautiful notebook you are going to buy to record your work is a list of people who may be affected by your decision to follow this process. Ask yourself, do they know about and/or support you in this journey? List three ways in which they will benefit by your following this process and list three ways in which they may be threatened by your following this process. Finally, list ten simple ways you can minimise any unpleasant impact for these people. Include in this list the times you will choose to communicate (not when they have just walked in the door from a hard day's work) and the voice you will use (not the 'you have to change now' one).

Silent success speaks volumes

One of the simplest ways to minimise fallout is to keep your own counsel. Being self-contained is a direct line to a more effective life in all areas, especially financial. By self-contained I don't mean the kind of false reticence that keeps money from being discussed frankly and openly, a malaise that is all too common in our society with damning repercussions. I mean the kind of confident assuredness that does not need constant expression or external reinforcement. Perhaps you are involved with someone whose financial attitude and behaviour has an impact on you. Let's say for example that you would like them to 'adapt' to your new approach. The most effective way to help them is to help yourself first. Great results speak louder than any lecture or coercion. Let your new-found financial acumen and confidence do the talking. It may appear to take a moment longer to be heard, but silent success speaks volumes and inspires devoted imitation.

YOUR FINANCIAL HISTORY

Enough about other people, let's get back to you. You come here today with your own money story. We all have our own money recipe. A handful of personal characteristics, one to two large helpings of parental influence, a dollop of concentrated peer pressure, a dash of societal mindset, a spoonful of good and/or bad experiences to taste, baked in a hot oven of cultural distinctions and all mixed into one big melting pot of personal financial psychological soup. If your recipe is to your taste, great. Keep it. If it doesn't then why on earth would you keep baking the same dish? Dump it and rewrite one that you love. Over the next chapters, we will be examining the ingredients of your personal financial recipe, throwing out the flavours you dislike and trying out new mixtures until you find your favourite. Let's get started. Here's your first set of exercises. Good luck!

THE WORK

1. Spend some money. Buy the best notebook you can afford. Preferably find one that has columns for calculating numbers such as a cashbook. Buy one that makes you feel rich when you look at it and sensuous when you touch it. Make sure you can easily afford it so that you also feel comfortable when you look at it. Make it the first purchase of your new financial life. Take it to your own personal Parisian café, buy your favourite coffee and begin by answering the following questions.

2. Why you, why now? What would you like your financial future to look like? Answer the following questions to help you paint the picture. Write your answer in ten minutes or less.

- What will it mean to you if you change your financial habits now and take charge of your financial life starting now?
- What will it really mean for your future to be comfortable and confident in handling your money?
- Who do you want to become financially?
- What things will you be able to give yourself and those you care for?
- What experiences will you be able to have and what experiences will you be able to share with others?
- Close your eyes for a moment and see yourself in

twelve months having taken control of your money. How does that feel?

- See yourself in five years and ten and twenty years. What does that look like?
- How will your life be different if you are financially competent and confident?
- What will your financial future look like if you keep on the way you are going? Answer all the same questions again but this time see yourself in twelve months *not* having taken control of your money. What does that picture look like? How does that feel? Describe where you will be in five years and ten and twenty years if you do not change your financial habits now. Again, write your answer in ten minutes or less.

3. Your money and your mind. Answer the following questions in your notebook.

- What did you learn from your father about money?
- What did you learn from your mother about money?
- What did you learn about money at school?
- Are the people who shaped you financially, financially secure themselves?
- What patterns do you have around money that get you into trouble?
- What does money mean to you?
- What do you believe about yourself and money?

4. Love where you're at while you get where you are going. Draw a line on a page from left to right and mark a scale of 0–100 per cent, where 0 is utter dissatisfaction with your finances and 100 is total satisfaction with your finances. Make a mark at your current level of satisfaction. List the elements of your financial life with which you are satisifed. Perhaps you already have a steady income. Perhaps you have bought things in the past that you love. Perhaps you have few or no debts. Take a moment to acknowledge and be grateful for the pieces of your current financial situation that you like.

5. Take a break. I know you have only just started, but listen, we've already agreed to do this the easy way. So your last exercise is to go and have a laugh. Whatever does it for you, take a bike ride in the park with a friend or have a martini in your dressing-gown with high heels. Be outrageous, be like money, be fun.

Key idea

If you don't understand your finances, they just haven't been explained to you properly yet.

2
Know Your Worth

You cannot motivate the best people with money.
Money is just a way to keep score. The best people in
any field are motivated by passion

ERIC S. RAYMOND

Wherever you are right now, stop and look up. Look around you or out of the window if you are at home. I want you to take a look at the first person you see. That probably took all of thirty seconds. Now look again and this time watch yourself watching them. What exactly do you see? Be aware of your thought processes. Listen to yourself talking about them in your head. Pay attention in particular to the automatic assessments you make while you look.

It all happens so quickly, you barely had to glance up. If I were to ask you what you think you now know about that person, what would you tell me? Take a moment consciously to go over what you have unconsciously told yourself about that person and the details of their life from that one cursory glance. You probably assessed their hair, the cut and the style, the colouring and whether it was neglected or well groomed and decided whether they might go to an expensive salon regularly or do their own home colouring. You checked out their skin and decided whether they spend money on skin care or skin products. You possibly even noticed their level of dental health. You probably decided on the quality of their diet, whether they eat healthily or cram junk food and whether they exercise or not. There's a glance over their clothes taking in the quality and labels.

Their jewellery and choice of bag, if any, provide more clues, leather or cloth, years old and bashed up or smart and shiny new. And you finish with a fleeting glance at their feet, taking in their shoes, all the while listening to their accent and vocabulary if you can hear them and noting their mannerisms. You know it's true. In a mere thirty-second intake, we make an assessment of what kind of work that person might do, where they fit on the socio-economic scale, the level of education they may have had and the type of background they may have come from. At the same time we decide whether they belong to 'our group' of people or not.

HOW DO YOU KEEP COUNT?

When we are done assessing our neighbours by the way they look, we move on to their homes and their lifestyle. What kind of car do they drive, do they holiday abroad or at home, or at all, how often do they change their car, what kinds of schools do their children go to, what kind of Christmas presents do they give their children, how often do they go out? The list is endless and we have an automatic scoring board in our heads that keeps everyone in their correct pecking order. It all adds up to figuring out who is better off than whom, and, consequently, who is 'better' than whom.

Why and how we came to use this system of assessment is the subject of the excellent *Status Anxiety* by Alain de Botton. In this incisive and often hilarious book, he explores how and why as a culture we came to equate the external trappings of wealth with someone's worth. He tracks the allocation of prestige in our culture through the days of hereditary privilege to today's system of 'meritocracy'. Where once your position and indeed worth was dependent on the family you were born into, in today's system, 'where prestigious and well-paid jobs could be secured only on the basis of one's own intelligence and ability, it now seemed that wealth might be a sound sign of character. The rich were not only wealthier, they might also be plain *better*.'

No wonder we look to material and financial success to decide if someone is *worth* our while or *worth* knowing. If everyone has the same chances in life, the same opportunities for education, advancement and success, then it follows that those who display material wealth are smarter, more competent, better judges of character and deals, more capable, more learned, better educated and therefore worth more of our time and respect. We are fair about it. It's not just our neighbours we assess in this way. We apply the same criteria to ourselves in turn to see if we are matching up to our (and our neighbours') expectations. Within each social stratum, there is a silent material checklist of what represents success, achievement and ultimately worth (think of how many times you have seen the executive progress from BMW to Mercedes to Jaguar if you need any reminding). It's a deeply ingrained habit, so ingrained it has become just the way things are.

What if I told you that these criteria, which we use to judge someone's material wealth and therefore their 'worth', are exactly wrong; that counting up the external signs of someone's material wealth tells you absolutely nothing about how well they are doing materially or financially. In fact, what if I told you that the more signs of wealth you see, quite possibly, the worse off they are doing financially. All these supposed signs of wealth don't tell you how much your neighbours owe, or if they are struggling to make the minimum payments on what they owe. They don't tell you how many years of their future earnings they have promised to hand over to the car leasing and mortgage companies which still have to be paid at a future date. They don't tell you if they inherited money they did not actually earn with their supposed extra competencies. And they certainly don't tell you how many sleepless nights they may have over their financial commitments.

DON'T BE FOOLED BY FALSE WEALTH

The sad thing is that the means of displaying wealth that we are conditioned to accept are actually contrary to real wealth-building. Put simply, really wealthy people do not waste their money trying to look as though they are wealthy. They are not out buying more and more 'better' things. They know that material things alone do not measure real wealth. Certainly there is an element of being able to buy the possessions that make life more comfortable, but real wealth means being lifestyle wealthy as well as financially wealthy. It means valuing yourself first and foremost, whether you have a brass farthing or not. It means owning what you value and valuing what you own and not merely consuming goods without having time to savour the taste of proud ownership before rushing on to chase the next item.

Imagine tomorrow morning you wake up and you find your neighbours, the Joneses, out on the patio, barbecue fired up, preparing for a big family brunch. You look on a little enviously; maybe you don't have a patio yet. And then you notice what is on the menu: money. They are burning their money. There they are having a few glasses of punch and putting bundles of cash on the fire, turning it carefully to make sure it all gets burned, chatting and laughing. What is your level of envy now? Do you immediately want to rush out and put bundles of money on your barbecue? Don't you want to keep up with the Joneses? Or do you suddenly have an urge to move as far away as possible from these lunatics who obviously have no sense, and clearly no sense of the value of money. Surely these cannot be the people who represent the supposed excellence of character and judgement that wealth is supposed to represent?

> Really wealthy people do not waste their money trying to look as if they are really wealthy

As a culture we are encouraged to burn our way through our money in a desperate attempt to show our worth to the world, but in reality the moment you spend your money on something (unless it is an investment, such as an antique or a piece of collectable art), it no longer contributes to your wealth. It's like the fable of the emperor with no clothes. We have become conditioned to think that the more things we see our neighbours buy, the better they are doing and the more we need to keep up. But in this case the emperor is not naked, he's more likely to be wearing clothes he can't afford or hasn't paid for. As the UK hits a national debt of one trillion pounds, the consequences of thinking that truly wealthy people display their wealth in this way, and, worse, of thinking that this is how we too must demonstrate that we are increasingly wealthy and worthy, is threatening to individual wealth and the national economy.

REAL WEALTH

So what is a true measure of wealth? In financial terms it is simply how much money you keep. How can you tell this by looking at your neighbours? You can't. That is why real wealth is discreet, that is why you probably overlook your truly wealthy neighbours who don't have the latest gear or the brand-new car. You have been conditioned to think that they aren't doing so well because they only drive a second-hand car or have a twenty-year-old kitchen. But in fact, you could be entirely wrong; they might simply be keeping more of their money and sleeping better at night. Somehow that seems like the smarter, more competent option to me.

Last year, I was deeply saddened to read an article

about UK economics. Economists were concerned that the 'striving classes' might be in danger of stopping 'striving' and that this would be disastrous for the economy. This was the first time I had heard of the 'striving classes.' Who are they? It seems that they are you and me. They are ordinary men and women who want to do the very best they can for themselves and their families. They are hard-working, decent, committed people who go out day after day to earn money to spend on building better homes, providing better education, driving better, safer cars and creating better communities. They are the Joneses.

The Joneses aren't bad people, they are just people who want things to be better than they are. And what's wrong with that? Nothing! We all have our Joneses, and we are all somebody else's Joneses. Apparently, if the striving classes stop striving, then the economy slows down. So it's important that they don't stop. Everything must be done by the powers that be to encourage the striving classes to want more and more things. Then they have to continue to go out and earn the money to pay for those things and when that fails, to borrow money and work even harder and longer to pay it back with interest. These striving families across the country are encouraged to put themselves under immense stress to appear to be doing better than they are. Not too much better, just enough to steal their time and energy, just enough to encourage them to spend their money unwisely, just enough to ensure that they will have to go out and strive again tomorrow and the next day and the next day and the next, until they are too tired to care any more or until their families have moved on to start their own striving and the cycle begins again.

Stop striving, start living

I don't think that's good enough. And as you are reading this book, you have clearly come to the same conclusion. I'm no economist but it does seem to me to be unfair that millions of people are living in distress, under pressure and in fear, that families are spending more time thinking about how much they have to earn and how much they owe, than about how much they love each other. There must be a better way of feeding the economy than with the blood, sweat and tears of the majority of the population. We've all been exposed to celebrity and millionaire rags-to-riches stories but what is the potential for building wealth for those who have simply gone through school, passed their exams, gone into their professions or jobs or businesses, had their families, bought their houses and are busy getting on with life, people like you and me? Can you become wealthy without being a six-foot beauty, or launching a revolutionary web product? And if so, how?

Actually it's surprisingly easy. The first thing to do is

step off the expensive appearances merry-go-round. Accept that having more possessions does not mean you are necessarily smarter with your money or are a better person, or worth more to society. When you decide that you are worthwhile as a human being just because you exist and regardless of what you own, you can begin to use your money your way. That brings with it an amazing combination of security and freedom: the security of believing in and trusting yourself, and the freedom to make choices dictated by your own needs. When you don't care what the neighbours think (in the nicest possible way) you are free to make your own choices.

HONESTY IS STILL THE BEST POLICY

When it comes to bringing your self-worth back inside yourself, honesty and integrity are two of the elements you want to nurture. Striving to keep up appearances is all about showing yourself as you would like to be perceived to be rather than just as you are, the inference being that who you are is not worth enough without the trappings. When you speak about money do you talk your worth or the worth you would like to be perceived to have? Do you for example sometimes say that something cost more than it did or less than it did depending on who you are talking to? Do you buy things on sale but pretend that you paid full price? Do you spend more on gifts than you can honestly afford because that's what the receiver will expect? Have you picked up the bill for a group lunch when you did not really have the money?

From now on I want you to commit to bringing honesty and integrity to all your language about money. Get specific, be honest, no fudging. If the item cost £9.99 say £9.99 not £10 or £5. It might be a bit scary at first. You might feel a little vulnerable without the protection of vague allusions to supposed wealth. But there is an elegance in honest vulnerability. This doesn't mean you go around declaring to the world that your car is actually on a lease agreement when you have usually alluded to owning it. Be self-contained. Keep your own counsel. Talk less but when you speak, speak honestly. This will do more to ground your true self-worth than you could possibly imagine.

YOUR FINANCIAL NET WORTH

That just leaves you free to manage your actual financial worth and that's the easy part. The only true measure of financial progress is tracking your 'net worth'. This simply means that every so often you stop, count up everything you own, subtract everything you owe, and *voilà*, you have your 'Statement of Net Worth'. Net worth is best calculated at least annually. However, in the beginning of learning about your finances I recommend redoing it every six months or even quarterly. Do it also when you are making major decisions. Calculating your net worth is like taking a photograph. It stands still in time. And the powerful thing about this is that you can see from photo to photo what has changed. It's a bit like playing 'spot the difference'. You can see if something has been added or taken away from one photo to the next. Financial progress is when your net worth figure gets higher year by year. When the figure increases it tells you that you are keeping some of the money you are making.

Separating your self-worth from your material possessions is one of the greatest gifts you can give yourself. Start now. Calculate your financial net worth and put it aside as a figure that represents nothing more than your financial progress. Concentrate on who you are as a human being when you want to assess your personal worth. Don't let yourself or anyone else persuade you ever again that the two are linked.

THE WORK

1. Examine your neighbour, examine yourself. Pick a neighbour or friend to whom you regularly compare yourself and consciously run through your assessment of them. Write down the assumptions you have made about their wealth, or lack of it, about the way they manage their money or don't. What things have you made assumptions about? What do you really know about what they earn or spend or borrow? What don't you know? Now do the same for yourself. See yourself in your mind's eye and write the assumptions you wish to project about what you earn or are worth to others. How do you project and protect those appearances? What is the truth?

2. Calculate your Statement of Net Worth. This exercise should take you less than two hours in total although you may have to wait for some of your questions to be answered. You need to pick one day (today sounds good) and add up everything you own and everything you owe on that day. Round off numbers to the nearest £. Estimate conservatively. If you are not sure of a value, make a good guess. Getting the picture 90 per cent correct and finished is better than aiming for 100 per cent accurate and never getting there.

		£
	Statement of Net Worth for_____ **Date**:	
	Assets (everything you OWN)	
A	**Investment in real estate** *(do not include your own home; write the current market value)*	
B	**Investment in business and partnerships** *(the current market value)*	
C	**Art, collectables, etc.**	

continued overleaf

D	**Monies owed to you** *(debtors)*	
E	**Pension plan** *(current surrender value; if your plan does not allow you to surrender, put zero)**	
F	**Life insurance** *(current surrender value)**	
G	**Stocks, bonds** *(current market value)*	
H	**Cash** *(count all the cash you have in your pockets, purse and piggy bank and enter the total)*	
I	**Cash equivalents** *(total bank accounts, credit unions, money market accounts, post office)*	
J	**Your principal, private residence** *(current market value of your home)*	
K	**Personal belongings** *(things you own such as jewellery, furnishings, cars, etc. estimated at what you would actually receive if you had to sell them all today)*	
L	**Total Assets** *(Add lines A–K) (the value of everything you OWN if you had to sell it all today)*	
	Liabilities (everything you OWE)	
M	**Accounts payable** *(outstanding bills such as electricity or telephone, which you have used but have not yet paid)*	

continued on next page

N	**Business loan** *(any monies that you may have been loaned to put into a business)*	
O	**Credit cards** *(write the total amount you owe on each credit card)*	
P	**Lines of credit** *(this includes hire purchase or lease agreements such as for your car and shop credit such as store cards)*	
Q	**Personal debts** *(monies owed to friends and family)*	
R	**Mortgages on investment properties**	
S	**Mortgage on your principal, private residence**	
T	**Total Liabilities** *(Add lines M–S) (the value of everything you OWE if you had to pay it all today)*	
U	**NET WORTH** *(Subtract line T from line L) (IF you were to sell everything you own today, pay all your debts and walk away with all you possess financially in your pockets, it would be this amount)*	

* The surrender value is the amount you would receive if you cashed in the plan today. Not all plans can be cashed in before their term is up.

3. Catch yourself doing well? Right now, with your Statement of Net Worth in front of you, you are the proud owner of something that only 5 per cent of the population have – the financially secure 5 per cent. This marks the spot where you have committed to your financial future. Take a moment to be proud of yourself.

4. Appreciate pricelessness. Visit a beautiful park or go somewhere with amazing views you love. Watch children playing and laughing in a playground, smell a rose or listen to a wonderful piece of music. Examine how it feels to look at, hear and do things that are worth so much but which cannot be bought with money. What is priceless for you in your life? It could be as simple as five minutes of peace and quiet with a perfect cup of tea and your favourite magazine. Keep a list of your priceless moments and plan to indulge in them as often as you can.

5. Be worthy. Do something for someone this week. To increase your internal feeling of worth and separate it from material possessions, do worthy things. Spend an extra few moments with a child who wants your attention or help an old lady with her bags. Whatever pops up for you, take the opportunity to remind yourself how worthy you are.

Key idea

When your self-worth is no longer dependent on your net worth, that is the true definition of financial freedom.

3

Know What You Spend

*There was a time when a fool and his money were soon
parted, but now it happens to everyone*

ADLAI STEVENSON

This is my favourite part, the part where you get to
decide what you really would love to spend your
money on. I enjoy making money, and I really enjoy
spending money. Spending should form a large part of
any self-respecting adult's financial habits, whether it's
on the fabulous car you drive, the clothes you wear, the
courses you attend, the travel you experience, the security you provide for your family or the contribution you
make to society. Unfortunately, with traditional financial planning, this is the part where an 'expert' looks
down a long list of your expenses, tells you what you
are allowed to keep, what you have to give up and how

much that will help towards paying for your nursing home care when the time comes. I don't know about you, but being told what I cannot do, however well intentioned, does not inspire me and working within some dull, grey budget is not going to get me through a bad day. I don't believe in diets and that includes financial diets. I believe in possibilities.

I have noticed over the years that when someone comes for financial coaching, if their goal is just to fix their money problems, they often find it tough to stay the course. The goal of managing money in itself is not enough to sustain the spirit of a person for any length of time. However, if someone comes with their goal being to take a year off and travel, or to buy the dream car they have always wanted, and in order to do so they have to sort out their money problems, it's different. These people usually fly through the programme and are soon heading off towards their dreams equipped with a new financial structure and approach to help them achieve their dreams more quickly and directly.

SPENDING SHOULD BE FUN

So as we begin to look at how to make your spending work for you, I have only one rule. Your spending plan must make you feel really good. Every time you think of spending money, I want you to have a smile on your face. And every time you choose not to spend your money, I want to see that same smile. There must be no sense of doing without. The feeling of doing without is contrary to the feeling of abundance and choice that underpins true wealth. How will you know when you have it right? You will smile. It's like finding the perfect gift for someone you love. You know that feeling you have when you see something that might seem silly or of no importance except that you know someone who will love it. Even if the item costs just pennies. As you think of the person's face when you give it to them, you can't help a huge grin appearing on your own face. That's the feeling you are looking for; nothing less will do.

I am fully aware that it can also be frightening to begin to look at what you spend, especially if your finances are out of control. Take heart. It is less frightening to know than not to know, I promise. It is the unknown that renders you powerless and steals your strength and focus. Once you know the facts, you will find solutions for any problems just popping up. There are exercises at the end of this chapter designed to help you find out your spending figure, to identify your spending patterns and to create new ones that support you. So all you need to do is follow the steps one at a time. We'll get there together.

WHAT MAKES YOU SPEND?

Before we get on to the exercises, I want to talk about *how* you spend. It's one thing to know what you spend; it's another to explore why you spend. Ultimately it's the why that drives the how and if you have spending patterns that are not supporting you, or in other words if your spending is out of control, then bringing it back under your management is incredibly empowering.

Picture the scene. It's another ordinary day, the sky is dull, and you are on your way to work and your bus or taxi slows in the traffic. Out of the window, you catch a glance of the most fabulous outfit, and it's reduced in 'today's greatest ever, everything must go, one-day sale.' Right away you are mentally wearing the new outfit, heads are turning, gasps of admiration and not a little envy are heard as you glide past. That special someone finally sees you with new eyes and cannot resist. The car behind hoots the horn, your driver mouths a list of expletives and you are jolted back to your dull morning and the long day ahead.

It's very clever. There you were getting on with your day, semi-happy with your lot, not giving a second thought to what you didn't have. Now you are very unhappy and, worse, in this dissatisfied state of mind you have to find the strength to deny yourself something you have just enjoyed in your mind. It took seconds mentally to see yourself buying that outfit, wearing it and hearing yourself getting the perfect reactions. Now you have long painful hours looking at your old worn-out clothes, which seemed fine this morning, but now you see only what is wrong with them. It's hard convincing yourself, in the face of such evidence, that you can't have or don't need the gorgeous outfit.

> **Stop** right there! This is the moment you must learn to recognise

All day long we are bombarded with fabulous pictures of flawless skin, perfect bodies, sleek cars, happy families and sunkissed beaches. It's no wonder that we look at our own possessions, our own lives and feel that they are somehow 'less than'. This is the moment when you are no longer your own decision-maker. I know you might appear to be. After all, you are the one who is going to decide to get a taxi at lunchtime and go back to the shop and buy the outfit. You are going to 'decide' that you are going to find the money to pay for it. But let's take a deeper look at what is really going on.

Someone else interrupted your day, at their choice of time and location and offered you something you were not actively looking for. Then when they had your attention, they told you that if you didn't buy it now, you wouldn't get the same deal tomorrow – you will miss out. In one fell swoop, you were offered something, allowed to feel the wonderful emotions that having it would bring and threatened with having it taken away again all in the same instant. It's very clever, very powerful and very difficult to resist.

Don't just spend something, stand there

When I was studying to become an on-line trader, I came across one piece of wisdom that made me more money than any other piece before or since. It was a comment from one of the wise old grandfathers of trading. It was simple: 'Make your decisions when the market is closed.' What this meant is that before the market opened, I should know what stock I wanted to buy or sell and at what price. Whatever happened once the bell rang, up or down, I should only buy or sell if the right stock hit the right price target.

The stock market is a wildly emotional arena. It can swirl you on a ride of emotional highs and lows and spit you out the other side a shell of your former self if you let it. The advertising world will do the same. The triggers are more subtle, the ride is less intense, the consequences seem less serious, but the result is longer lasting. The long-term, chronic, low-level financial stress of being persuaded to buy something you may or may not really need or even want, is more insidious and life-draining than anything I have seen in the world's most demanding markets. To have spent your hard-earned money on something that does not give you lasting pleasure or, even worse, leaves you feeling guilty and dissatisfied is a cruel waste.

BE YOUR OWN DECISION-MAKER

Let's go back for a moment to that fabulous outfit you saw in the window. I want to tell you a true story that will change for ever the way you think about spending money. I want to show you how one lady bought more fabulous, more expensive clothes she really wanted for less money than all the cheaper clothes that didn't really suit her. For you guys this might not seem relevant but bear with me. On the one hand, men are now being targeted in the fashion and beauty world in a way that has been hitherto reserved for women. And if you're not interested in clothes chances are you are or will be involved with someone to whom they are important.

So, let's talk for a moment about clothes shopping. It's the bane of 90 per cent of women's lives. The sheer cost of looking great is daunting. For most of us it means ending up with a wardrobe full of clothes we don't wear, don't like and which don't do anything for us. They were someone else's idea of what would look good, be fashionable, be this season's must-have colour, looked good on the shop dummy, or whatever you were told the day you bought it. But the cost of these mistakes could fund so many real dreams. Clothes and looking good are the areas over which the media and advertising world seems to have the most power to make us spend our money.

ANN'S STORY

Ann came to me because she was feeling lousy. She and her husband did not really have money problems. They had two children and she was happy that she had the freedom to stay at home. But she was awkward with her new 'dependent' status and was feeling vaguely unproductive and unworthy and was uncomfortable spending her 'husband's money' on herself. Her self-esteem, which had been fed by her previous work and financial success, was at an all-time low. As we talked, it quickly became obvious that apart from not earning her own money, her loss of self-worth was exacerbated by the extra weight she had not shed since the birth of her second child and the dramatic change in her body shape post-pregnancy. From being a snappy size 8, fit and toned, she had gone to a saggy size 14 (not a good look for someone skimming five feet) and she had lost all interest in her appearance. She was lacking in energy and drive, was tired, had a demanding one-year-old and a toddler, and wore clothes that reflected the cloud that seemed to be hovering over her: grey, dull and shapeless. I felt that she needed a quick, fun lift more than she needed financial coaching.

We decided that she would first go to Clothesology. Clothesology is the brainchild of a wonderful lady who has the ability to look at a woman, see her at her most beautiful and show her how to dress herself to reflect that inner beauty. While many stylists 'style' and the result is the right colour, the right shade, the right hemline or neckline, the Clothesology process finds the connection between the inner woman and her clothes. It gets the result that most of us are actually searching for during our whole lives when we shop. Ann learned how to express herself through her clothes and then how to shop to find exactly the right things. It was nothing short of a miraculous transformation.

From one day to the next Ann glowed again and more powerfully than ever before. Now here's the thing. Ann spent a day going over her existing wardrobe à la Clothesology, another day learning how to plan her new wardrobe, then another day shopping. She paid a substantial professional fee for each day and she spent a good amount on new clothes. Altogether it was a significant investment. But the by-product of all this spending was that in the two years since Ann has not made one wasteful impulse buy. She has become immune to advertising and sales pitches and she has not bought anything she does not love and wear regularly. She learned to be her own decision-maker and she has saved more than double the amount she paid to

Clothesology. Now she clothes shops twice a year, with a planned shopping list, always looks comfortable and fabulous in her clothes and continues to spend less on her wardrobe year after year. Now that's a truly fabulous way to save money.

SPEND MORE TO SPEND LESS

Scrimping on your spending rarely works and certainly is not much fun, but spending your money well is an art that allows you to have what you really want and be better off for doing so. When you spend your money on items that reflect who you are and what is important to you, you value what you own and receive ongoing pleasure from your possessions. Happy people waste less money. They simply are not persuaded by the 'feel-good' fix promised by advertising. They don't need it, they feel good already. I'm not interested in cutting back and doing without to save money. I am interested in finding smarter ways to spend money so that I can have more fun and more free time to spend with my family and do and have the things I love. I am here to tell you that managing what you spend is not only smart and sensible but when you spend your money on the things that really matter to you, life sings.

CREATE YOUR OWN SPENDING PLAN

The first step in setting up your spending plan is to find out what you are doing currently. Let me ask you, How much do you spend exactly per month? If you have not given one exact specific figure by right now, then you don't really know. If your answer started with, 'Well, it depends' or 'Some months' or 'Last month' then it really is time to get to grips with this elusive number. Knowing specifically how much you spend per month is one of the most comfortable pieces of information you can carry in your head. Think of your favourite jeans, the ones that are worn to fit perfectly, faded and torn but every time you pull them on you just feel sooooo comfortable. Remember how it was finding those jeans in the first place. It takes some looking to find just the right ones, and then you have to wear them in. After a while your body shape moulds them to fit you better and before you know it, they are your old favourites.

That's how it feels to know how much your life costs you on a monthly basis. At first it's a little bit of a search to find out what the number might be, then you begin to wear it for a while and notice where it might need a little alteration or adjustment. And then one day it is just part of what you know and is like a guiding beacon in all financial decision-making that enables you to make even snap decisions from a place of power and clarity that affects your entire financial future. It is that important and that powerful.

HOW MUCH DO YOU CURRENTLY SPEND?

The first action item at the end of this chapter is designed to help you identify how much your life is currently costing you. In financial terms this exercise is about establishing your 'Expenses'. As you do this, be aware that listing your expenses is just one piece of a jigsaw of several pieces. Only when it is all put together can you see the picture clearly so don't make any rash decisions or get disheartened at this stage, no matter what the figures tell you. Round off numbers to the nearest pound. Estimate on the high side. If you are not sure of a cost, make a good guess. I have given you a list of items to jog your memory but replace these with your own personal list. Do not spend much time searching out exact figures; estimate and move through this exercise quickly. As you actually spend during the month ahead you can compare back to your estimates and update them until you have a more accurate picture.

MAKE YOUR SPENDING WORK FOR YOU

The fact that you are reading this book, however, suggests that what you are currently doing with your money is not working for you. So the next step is to look through your expense list and see how you are spending your money. In the second action item, the 4-way exercise, you are guided to divide your expense list into the following categories:

- MH – Must Haves
- NTH – Nice to Haves
- I – Investments
- DR – Debt repayments

MHS are those expense items without which your life would not function, such as food. NTHS are those items that you could do without if you had to, such as the newspaper. IS are those items that you pay from which you will receive some kind of return, such as pensions. DRS are payments you make towards any debts you may have.

Here is the key to MHS. We all have to pay our electricity bills and feed ourselves. And for some of you, you must have a car to get to work so your car, car tax and insurance are vital. But equally as important as feeding your body is feeding your mind and your spirit. You can give me three square meals a day every day but if I don't have a good book on the go life's not worth living. I jest, but only just. It is absolutely true that key to my health is a monthly massage. It releases stress, unblocks pains, prevents illness, re-energises me and is vital time out in this busy working mother's life. For me, a monthly massage is a Must Have. For someone else that may be a frivolity, for another person once a month would be draconian.

TREAT YOURSELF

The point is, you know what is vital to you. We will all have similar lists up to 90 per cent. The other 10 per cent will be individual and reflect who you are and what is important to you. What must you have in order to feel that you are living and not just existing? It may take a little while to get a handle on what is really important for you during the next weeks. Get used to standing back when you take out your wallet or are writing a cheque for something you are about to purchase. Stop and see what feelings you have around that spend. Ask yourself what is behind the decision to purchase this item, and make sure it is really your own choice. Allow your feelings of pleasure with your purchases to direct your choice of what goes on your spending plan.

'Yeah, right,' I hear you say, 'if I bought all the things that give me pleasure I'd need an open cheque from the Bank of England to pay for them.' So, let's be especially clear. A truly good feeling lasts, it does not give way to doubt or guilt when you get home. As important as respecting what would make you happy is assuming the responsibility that goes along with that. I'm not advocating that you start stomping your feet on the floor like a spoilt brat demanding the latest techno gadget just to express your inner child. If you want something and you need to have money to buy it, then it is important to be responsible about where that money is coming from. We'll be looking at that in later chapters; for the moment here are the first steps to creating your personal spending plan.

THE WORK

1. Calculate your current expenses. The easiest way to get the complete picture is to begin with your regular bills or your direct debits. Take each of these, for example your mortgage, and fill in the amount you pay each month. Then fill in the irregular items such as groceries with an estimate.

Monthly Expenses for _____ Date:	Amount	Category
Bank charges		
Books/mags		
Car insurance		
Car maintenance		
Car repayments		
Car tax		
Charitable contributions		
Christmas		
Clothing		

Continued overleaf

	Amount	Category
Dentist		
Electricity		
Fuel		
Garden		
Gas		
Gifts/presents		
Groceries		
Hobbies/sport		
Holidays		
House insurance		
House maintenance/décor		
Household equipment		
Investments (list each one)		
Kids' care		
Kids'clothing		
Kids'toys		
Legal/professional fees		
Medical bills		
Medical insurance		

Continued on next page

	Amount	Category
Pension		
Personal care		
Pet care		
Petrol		
Rates		
Rent/mortgage		
Restaurant		
School fees		
Stationery/postage		
Sundry expenses		
Telephone		
Travel		
TV licence		
Water		
Total Expenses		
Total Must Haves		
Total Nice to Haves		
Total Investments		
Total Debt Repayments		

2. Try the 4-way exercise. Now go through the list you have made and mark each item according to its level of importance to you.

- First identify all your MHs according to the notes in the chapter
- Then identify all your IS
- Next identify your DRS
- The remainder are your NTHS

Total each category and put them aside for now.

3. Check your comfort level. Your MH list should feel comfortable. If you begrudge paying your electricity, take a moment and remind yourself what life would be like without it. There are many who do have to do without. Cultivate an attitude of gratitude and pay the bills you must pay with good grace.

4. Find the smile. Look at each item in your NTH list and see if it makes you smile. If it doesn't, consider why you would continue to spend your money on it. Decide not to buy this item any more. This includes items that make you feel good for a while but about which you end up feeling guilty or resentful.

5. Have fun. As you move from your current expenses to your new spending plan, be flexible. You might find that you thought that you could not live without eating lunch out every day but in reality you are noticing that if you did not spend that money, you would be able to have something else you would prefer at the end of the week. If you thought you could give up your cigarettes but you're really missing them, put them back in.

Key idea

The shortest route to financial contentment is to spend more on the things that make you happy and nothing on the things that don't.

4

Know What You Earn

*It is better to have a permanent income
than to be fascinating*

OSCAR WILDE

Behind the winking windows of the tower blocks of Manhattan, fury erupted when it was discovered that a personal assistant had stolen over $5 million from two of her bosses' personal accounts. It had taken them five years to notice that the money was missing. One of them had lost $3 million from one account and still had not missed the money! How on earth could such a thing happen? How could someone earn so much money that they would not miss $3 million? If that shocks you, would you believe that far from Wall Street in ordinary homes across the country are people who have no idea what they earn?

DANIELLE'S STORY

Danielle was a typical example. A strong, capable woman, she has a vision for her life that she pursues with focus and determination. However, despite being a beautiful thirty-something, a successful business-woman and an accomplished athlete, she had grown up in a family where one did not discuss how much one earned. As a result, she ignored this side of her money management and it began to fail to support the dreams she was so successfully achieving. At least once a year she hit a cash-flow crisis and she would have to forgo something she planned. This fed her fears that she might not be doing as well as she thought.

Like many people who become self-employed, Danielle had no formal training in accounts. She was just doing what she loved. When we tied down exactly what she was making, she was stunned to learn how well she was doing. In the next twelve months, with new-found confidence in her continuing earning capacity underpinning her existing business acumen, she bought her first home and her first investment prop-erty. She also changed plans to expand one aspect of her business because she realised from her precise figures that by expanding another area of her business instead she would increase her earnings more. Once she knew how much she was earning, she began to plan how much she wanted to earn next. As I write she is on a three-week meditation retreat in Tuscany to reflect on exactly where she wants to take her life next. Then we'll work out what income will best support those plans.

FOCUS ON YOUR INCOME

I realise that not taking time to know what you are earning may seem like a luxury problem. For most the problem is the apparently more stressful one of simply not earning enough. But not knowing what you earn, whether you have too much income or not enough, generates the same state of unease. Have you made enough to pay the bills? What if there is a crisis, will there be cash available? Oddly, both situations pose the same questions, generate the same fears and the solution to both is the same. You must know exactly what you earn.

When it comes to money management the immediate instinct is to focus on expenses and take charge of where money is going. I believe it is even more important to focus on income. I encourage all my clients to spend at least an equal amount of time analysing their income. I want them to take a good look at whether or not their earnings are giving them the income they need and indeed if their earnings are commensurate with what they think they should be earning or what they feel they could be earning.

HOW MUCH DO YOU EARN?

Many people know exactly what they earn. They get a pay slip at the end of the month telling them. If this is you, how much do you earn? Write the figure down now and put it to one side. However, if you are not in employment, it might not be so clear. If you have inconsistent or irregular income you may not be sure exactly what your income is. In this situation it's even more important to pin down that vital number. We'll be doing that in this chapter.

There are three parts to the income issue.

1. Do you know what you earn?
2. Is it enough?
3. What would your ideal income be?

While many know the first and most have a nagging dissatisfaction with the second, few ever take the time (beyond wishful thinking) to sit down and decide on the third. Of those few who do, fewer still take the necessary actions to make that a reality.

Let's take it step by step. Step one is to find out what your current income is. Just follow the instructions at the end of this chapter to get to this figure for you. If you are one of those people who have a simple scenario with a payslip to tell you what you earn, go back and look at the figure you wrote on the piece of paper earlier in this chapter. Did you write your gross earnings; that is the figure that includes your tax? Or did you write the net amount, which is the amount you have left after your tax has been deducted?

BE CONSISTENT

It's only a one-word difference but it's a big one and it's one of the ways I have seen people kid themselves about their income. When they want to feel good about how much they're earning, they'll talk about their gross income. When they want to beat themselves up, they'll talk net. When they want to make themselves look good they'll allude to gross salary plus variable commissions, plus the bonus they got one extraordinary year. The danger is then believing that this one-off figure is the amount they make on a consistent, regular basis. There's no problem with painting a great picture to inspire yourself; there is a problem when everyday reality gets confused with a one-off.

Whatever way you communicate to yourself be clear about what is and what is not included in your income figure from today. When tracking your income use the same criteria each time you calculate your progress. Are you including pension contributions deducted automatically from your salary? Do you receive tax credits or child benefits? Add them in or don't but be consistent. This gives you a clear figure to work with which will underpin your financial management and planning.

DO YOU EARN ENOUGH?

What happens if the figure you are making is just not enough? Let's talk about step two. Are you making enough? How much is enough? Let's look at it practically first. Does your income cover your expenses? That is one basic form of enough. Begin with your 'Must Have' total from the last chapter. Does your income cover those basic requirements? Now what about your debt repayments if you have any? Does it cover those too? Next, look at your investments. What about your Nice to Haves? Which level of expenditure does your income meet or surpass? If there is a shortfall, use these as targets to calculate your first financial goals beginning with your Must Haves. If your income does not meet your outgoings, you will need to address this one financial issue before you can take on other financial goals.

I know there are many people who choose to sacrifice income in the short term to pursue their dearest dreams. I believe in dreams and in your right to pursue your dreams as a priority. If you are willing to do without in the short term so that you have more time to devote to your dreams, that is a valid choice and one that works well if you find the right comfort level for you. This approach does not work so well if you ignore your commitments or load up on credit, hoping that somehow you will make ends meet while you pursue those dreams. The stress of having an income below your outgoings can strangle your dreams.

> Don't steal from your future to pay for your present

This happens in two ways. Stress about meeting your bills will stifle your creativity and leave you too tired to be alert to opportunities, hampering your business growth. Relying on credit to meet your personal bills in the early years can leave you loaded with debt when you do make it. Anita is a capable professional who opted out of the London life to set up her dream business in the country. She borrowed money to keep herself afloat while she got her new business going. However, by the time she got her business off the ground she was loaded with extra debt payments for her personal expenditure. The new business then needed to produce income beyond its natural growth curve to meet the demand. The pressure of paying yesterday's bills threatens to put her out of business today. We are still working on solutions for her, but she may have to sell her business or her home to meet her accrued personal commitments. She now realises that if she had accepted other work unrelated to her dream business, which she had been offered during the previous two years, far from slowing down the achievement of her dreams, it would have actually contributed to the stability of her success.

Make sure you create a win-win for your today and your tomorrow. Start where you are and set things up so you have the money to pay your current bills, as well as keep your mind free and fresh while you pursue your dreams. Take that part-time job, accept the short-term contract, meet your current commitments while you pursue your deepest desires. You'll be glad you did.

ARE YOU EARNING YOUR FINANCIAL WORTH?

What about the underlying feeling you have about your income? Do you feel satisfied or dissatisfied? Do you feel that you are worth more than you are earning? If you work for yourself, do you feel happy with the amount you charge for your product or services? I have lost count of the times someone has provided me with an excellent service and then blushed and mumbled something apologetically when I asked how much I owe. Time and again I find clients' financial histories dotted with examples of delivering work but not having sent the invoices or of providing a service without setting out clear terms and then being in a difficult position when it comes to billing. Among employees, I find examples of people being so glad to have the chance to prove themselves that they accept a small starting salary and are then stuck with a yearly incremental increase from there.

PETER'S STORY

When Peter came to me for help with his debt he had been working at his job very successfully for three years. However Peter's salary had not increased significantly from his original graduate entry amount. To make ends meet, Peter bought 'Must Haves' on credit, one debt led to another and soon he was in trouble. He was a competent individual and in another situation he would have commanded an excellent salary that would have easily covered his simple lifestyle. But working in an environment where he was not recognised economically for his skills had penetrated his self-worth over the years and, coupled with his financial problems, he no longer had the confidence to put himself back into the job market. We needed a financial plan that he could manage on his existing salary, a tough challenge but one we met successfully. As the months went by, Peter would e-mail me to let me know how he was doing and I could see his confidence growing with each debt he cleared. As he achieved each financial milestone, his sense of self-worth increased and with it a growing frustration with his income. When he called to say he had posted his details with recruitment agencies I knew his income problems were over.

SELF-WORTH IS PRICELESS

Issues of self-worth show up in the income column. The common approach to resolving issues of insufficient income is to focus on finding another situation with a higher income. There are a number of ways to maximise your income. You can work for a promotion or a rise or get trained for another higher paid position. You can offer to work overtime, or start a business or second income stream part time. If you are self-employed you can raise your hourly rate, work more hours or offer more services. These are just simple ways. There are lots of creative ways to increase your income specific to you. While these are all worthy actions, in my experience focusing on the money alone is a short-sighted approach. Sooner or later the new income is not enough either.

> More money rarely solves money problems

The secret to a lasting solution can be found tucked away in the *Oxford Dictionary* of all places. The *Concise Oxford Dictionary* defines the verb to earn as follows:

EARN: (of a person) obtain (income) in the form of money in return for labour or services. *Deserve;* be entitled to; obtain as the reward for hard work or merit.

It is the sub-definition that caught my eye. To earn is to deserve. If you focus on the feeling of being deserving first, then your income issues will find themselves becoming resolved in a more satisfying and fulfilling way. In Peter's case, I could have tried to convince him that he was worth a higher salary right at the start. But even if he had been up to looking for a higher paying job he would have brought his sense of unworthiness to an interview. I would have done him a disservice, that of not letting him grow his own sense of self-worth. When he began to have small successes on his own merit he began to believe in himself again. That is priceless.

EARN YOUR OWN RESPECT

If your current income is not enough, certainly begin to consider how you might practically increase the figure. But, more importantly, begin treating yourself better. Do more of what you love and less of what you don't enjoy. Find ways to show yourself that you are worth more. Honour and respect yourself in small affordable ways. Say no when you want to. Speak well of yourself; that costs nothing. Stop grabbing a handful of moisturiser on the run; sit down to put on your face cream in the morning and smile at yourself in the mirror. Take small steps and grow gently into your sense of worth again.

You will be amazed at the wonderful feeling that spreads through your body when you treat yourself well. Notice the riches in your life such as your friends and family, the water that comes from your tap every day or the sheer amount of money circulating in the world. If your income is not sufficient for your current needs, I'm willing to bet you spend a significant amount of time noticing the lack and poverty around you. From now on, I want you to focus on noticing examples of plenty. Challenge yourself to find at least five examples every day, one of which must be in your own situation.

HOW MUCH DO YOU WANT TO EARN?

The last piece of the income puzzle, the most important, is knowing how much you want to earn. It's a simple fact that if you know this figure, clearly and specifically, there is actually a greater chance of earning it. Keep it real. There is no point in saying you'd like to earn £10,000 a month if your next thought is, 'As if'. I want you to begin to bring your income goals and your own feeling of what is possible into harmony, find that spot and begin from there. I know there are some well-documented stories of rags to riches, overnight successes. That's great and it could happen to you. There are also millions of undocumented stories of ordinary people who simply took one step at a time and achieved quiet success. While you are waiting for overnight success to strike, why not make sure your small steps are going in the same direction too. Then you win either way and you get the satisfaction of enjoying the journey instead of fretting while you hope for a miracle.

If you wanted to run a marathon tomorrow but had not done any running before, would you pump yourself up and attempt twenty-six miles on your first run? Of course not. You might go for a short run first and see how you got on. Then once you knew how much your body could handle you'd set training targets and go for practice runs, building towards the bigger goals. Money management is for life, and life is not a sprint. It's time to retrain.

BRIDGE THE GAP

When you think of how much you would like to earn, begin by thinking of how much you would like to earn next. Starting from where you are, look at your expense categories as detailed above. If your earnings cover all your expenses, consider a target of 10 per cent more than your expenses as your next income level. If you already have the 10 per cent consider 20 per cent. Put real figures on these targets. Ask yourself some simple questions. How much monthly income exactly would you like to earn? How much extra do you want to have to spend on items you want? As you consider each of these targets, I want you to watch out for when the 'As if' feeling rears its head. Stop there. When you don't really believe it's possible you place the biggest obstacle in your way:

yourself. If you have spent years telling yourself consciously or unconsciously that you can only earn so much, you need a few successes under your belt to give you a boost before you try for the high figures. The 'As if' feeling tells you when you have set a goal that is just a touch too far outside your current belief in yourself. Pull back a little until you feel comfortable and easy with a target that stretches you but does not stress you.

Harmonise your income goals and your belief in what is possible for you

---

When you set an income goal, make sure it is one you believe you can achieve and steadily focus on it until you get there. The success will spur you on and the subsequent goals will fall into place more and more easily. Even more importantly, you will enjoy the process. The fastest way to achieve your desires is to support them with confident expectation. Without the added ballast of believing your desire is achievable by you, now, you may vacillate between small successes and periods of doubt and downtime. You will still get there but the journey may take longer and be less enjoyable. When you confidently stride out in the direction of your goals knowing you will achieve each next one, you reduce your slippage and each small success builds on itself, creating a momentum that will kick in and carry you relentlessly towards your bigger targets.

Confident expectation is a wonderful ally. Cultivate it in every moment. As soon as the 'As if' thought hits, or the moment you feel self-doubt or fear, just stop. Don't move again until you have centred yourself. When in doubt, relax and get quiet within yourself. Don't try to chase goals when you are nervous or worried. A clear head and a clear focus will show you solutions you would never see when in fear or doubt. If you are not making the income you would like to be making, you first have to believe you deserve more, then take the practical steps necessary to add action to peaceful anticipation.

THE WORK

1. **Calculate your income.** List all sources of income and how much they provide. I have given you some headers, as it is easy to forget some less obvious items or not realise they should form part of your list.

Monthly income	
Salary	
Business income (net of expenses and taxes)	
Child benefit	
Tax credits	

continued on next page

Pension	
Investment income (net of taxes)	
Second job	
Dividends	
Total Monthly Income	

If your salary is irregular or commission-based, take your total annual salary for the last year (less any exceptional income that you might not usually have) and divide it by twelve.

2. Calculate your hourly rate. Take your monthly salary/income and divide it by the number of hours you work. Do not divide it by the number of hours you are supposed to work if you took all your lunch-breaks and went home on time every night. Divide it by the number of hours you *actually* work in an average month.

3. What are you really worth? Explore how you feel about your hourly rate. How does it make you feel? Are you being paid your worth? Is it smaller or greater than you expected? Is it less than you feel you are worth economically? Write in large red marker the figure you believe you should be paid per hour. Write twenty reasons why your work is worth that figure.

4. Telling your story. Take out the answers you gave to the 'Your money and your mind' exercise in Chapter 1. This is your financial story according to your most repeated memories. I want you now to rewrite that financial history and this time fill it with memories of abundance and plenty. For every memory you have of lack or mis-information about good money management, there are memories of moments of plenty and good lessons learned. You may have to dig a little harder to find these memories but I guarantee you they are there if you look. From now on, this new story is the story I want you to tell yourself.

5. Treat yourself well. Pick one thing that you would really love to have or do and incorporate it into your life. Find a way to do it now. If it is something you cannot yet afford, it is not the thing for you right now. Pick something you can do now, easily, with no strain financially or on your time. This is the fastest way to get that feeling that you think more income will give you. The better you treat yourself, the better you will feel about yourself, the more you will ask for yourself and from your life and the more life will give you.

Key idea

Treat yourself with respect and money will treat you with respect too.

5

Know What You Keep

*It's a kind of spiritual snobbery that makes people
think they can be happy without money*

ALBERT CAMUS

Why are you reading this book? Why do you want to learn about money? What is it all about? Are you spending your life in the pursuit of money for money's sake? I don't believe so. Most people are looking for a feeling they think will come with 'enough money.' Call it happiness, call it contentment, call it just the absence of stress or worry. Whatever name you give it, it's clearly not about the money itself. Sometimes we think we glimpse it on the faces of esoteric masters who spend their lives in contemplation, those who voluntarily go without the basic modicums of modern living, never mind the luxuries that we are persuaded to chase in search of that elusive contentment. So why don't we all just devote our lives to meditation and reflection and immerse ourselves directly in that feeling that we so desperately seek? Surely it's a foolproof short cut?

Despite the stresses and strains, most of us still want to live full lives in this real world. We have families we love and dreams we want to pursue. Sitting cross-legged on top of a mountain, however beautiful the view, while our children go without is not an option. We want to immerse ourselves in the throng of living and loving with our families and our friends. So how do you find that level of sheer satisfaction here in today's everyday life when everyone knows that first and foremost you must have a certain amount of money just to exist never mind pursue your highest goals? And, more especially, when the earning of that money takes up the majority of your time and attention, leaving meagre pickings of energy and interest for the finer things in life.

CHECK THE SIGNS

Could it be that you are simply looking in the wrong place? Could it be that you are looking into the distance for something that lies within arm's reach? What if the signposts of financial progress have been misprinted and are leading you on a journey that will never take you where you want to go? I read recently that the next generation of disillusioned young people is emerging. The sad thing is that this generation is getting disillusioned earlier than previous ones. Whereas we used to hang on to some kind of hope that things would work out until our mid-thirties, it seems that this dissatisfaction is now hitting in the mid-twenties. I am not surprised. As we go through life from school, through college and on to the career ladder or into business, working our way up through ever increasing notches of income, we forget or were perhaps never educated to realise that increasing income is yet another unsatisfactory signpost for any kind of success, least of all financial success. We have already discussed how we are conditioned to keep an eye on how much our neighbours are buying. We also watch for signs of what they might be earning. It would appear that we have not learned to balance the information about what is being earned with what we are all actually doing with that income once we have it. Increasing income alone is no guarantee or indicator of financial progress.

Imagine you go to your favourite shop and pick up a totally fabulous suit and you take it home. The next week you are invited to an event and as you mentally go through your wardrobe you decide that the suit is just perfect and decide that's what you will wear. Imagine your shock when you go to get ready that evening and, lo and behold, no suit in your wardrobe, just a cashmere jumper. On reflection, you remember that you had decided that the suit wasn't quite right and you took it back to the shop and exchanged it for the jumper. That would never happen with clothes of course. You would know that although you brought the suit home, you did not keep it and therefore it does not form part of your wardrobe. Even though it came into your home, that is not enough to make it part of your possessions. Once you exchanged it for something else, it was no longer yours.

Wealth is what you keep, not what you earn

But we do this all the time with money. We somehow count what comes into the household as how much we have, as if every penny we earn were contributing to building our wealth. 'Hey, I got a rise this year, I'm doing well financially.' Maybe so. But maybe not, and indeed probably not if national statistics are anything to go by. The only way the suit gets to be part of your wardrobe is if you keep it and the only money that counts as your wealth is the money you keep. Let me repeat this again. The only money that counts as your wealth is the money you keep. You can keep it in the bank, you can buy something that holds its value or increases in value such as property or antiques. Or you can just put it under your mattress. That all counts. But as soon as you exchange it for something you will consume today or something that will be worth less tomorrow, it does not count towards your wealth.

START SLOWER TO MOVE FASTER

Here's the second element of this truth. When you keep what you value and value what you keep, that elusive contentment you are chasing comes creeping in all of its own accord. It might take a moment to notice because we have been taught to look for the bright, sharp flash of quick excitement and gratification. Happiness and contentment are much softer visitors. However, like an addict chasing a drug high, we have been persuaded to chase the excited rush of the impulse buy of the latest gadget or piece of fashion as a replacement for the long-term, low-level contentment of having and using possessions we savour. It's the same as confusing the chocolate bar sugar high with the fresh, sustainable high energy of vital health. It might be more dramatic and more instant to get the quick fix, but it wears off very quickly, is less satisfying in the long term, and takes more and more of the original trigger to maintain the effect as time goes by.

It's a contradictory conundrum. By one school of thought we are persuaded that we must pursue earning money as a priority in life. And by another equally persuasive school of thought, we are reminded that money does not buy happiness. Early education and experience persuaded me to set up my life to earn money as a priority at the same time as believing, along with millions of others, that money does not equal happiness. So what's the point of pursuing money or having money or even learning about how to manage money if it doesn't make us happier than we have been? I've had the chance to be around very wealthy people and to be around very poor people and it has taken me forty-odd years, but I have come to believe that we've been duped by the contradictory arguments about money and happiness. I have come to believe that there *is* a direct link between happiness and money. The error was in assuming that if something makes us happy then more of it must make us happier. I believe we have missed the simplicity of the truth.

Show me an unhappy person who really needs £50, let me give them £50 and I'll show you immediate happiness. But show me someone who has millions and is unhappy despite great wealth, let me give them £50 or £50,000 and it will not alleviate their unhappiness one jot. It seems that money can bring happiness even if more money does not bring more happiness. I suspect that keeping a little of what you earn will make you happier than you can possibly imagine, especially if you have been living under financial strain. Beyond that, keeping significantly more than enough does not necessarily equate to significantly more happiness.

THE RELATIONSHIP BETWEEN MONEY AND HAPPINESS

It seems I'm not the only one who thinks so. A major survey of happiness in the US, carried out by economist

Richard Easterlin over almost three decades and published in 2003 through the Social Science Research Network, found that once a country achieves a certain level of economic development, its inhabitants don't necessarily get any happier the wealthier they become. After a certain point, he states, 'An increase in income, and thus in the goods at one's disposal, does not bring with it a lasting increase in happiness because of the negative effect on utility of hedonic adaptation and social comparison.' It seems that once we start to want and get goods just for the sake of having them or so that we can simply look good in front of others, satisfaction with the goods diminishes. He goes on to explain that allocating an excessive amount of time to pecuniary goals distracts us from spending time on non-pecuniary goals such as family life and health, further reducing levels of happiness. Another recent US study revealed that 37 per cent of a group of very rich people polled were less happy than the national average. Need I go on?

Some money does equal some happiness

It appears that, up to a certain point of economic success, there is a correlation between money and happiness. This is certainly borne out by my experience and one I have seen repeated among my clients. Allow me to show you how the relationship works as I have come to see it. Take, for example, a family whose monthly expenses are £2,000. If they earn even slightly more than £2,000 they are likely to be financially happy. If they earn anything less than £2,000 they are likely to be financially unhappy. If they earn much more than £2,000 their level of happiness does not necessarily continue to increase with each extra amount earned. It is my experience that the hottest, most emotionally charged income band is the 10–20 per cent just each side of the family total expenses.

Money and happiness

Monthly Income		Expenses £2,000
5,000		
4,000	No significant increase in happiness. Perhaps even mild to extreme unhappiness	
3,000		
2,000	Area of greatest happiness. Earning 10–20% more than your expenses	
	Area of greatest unhappiness. Earning 10–20% less than your expenses	
1,000	No significant increase in unhappiness. Perhaps even mild numbness to the situation	
0		

I will go even further. After years of personal fascination with the interplay between finance and emotion, I am still freshly amazed at the power of even just £100 on either side of the monthly expense total. It's as if that £100 band were quite simply filled with magic. Add it to the right side of your monthly accounts and it makes all the difference between a stressful month and a month of contentment. Deduct it from the wrong side of your accounts on a regular basis and it will throw you into the relentless downward spiral with which so many families currently struggle. On the right side of the equation it is magic, on the wrong side it is misery.

> I have yet to meet a client who cannot rearrange their finances to give themselves £100 of leeway in a month

While we hanker after the millionaire lifestyle of the celebrity, somehow assuming, despite all information to the contrary, that the wealth would bring contentment and freedom from our worries, the real solutions to our real issues lie right under our noses, easily accessible to everyone. I have yet to meet a client who cannot rearrange their finances to give themselves £100 of leeway in a month. More importantly, even where there is a significant challenge (take the example of a client with over

£30,000 debt and no income), the goal of finding an income that will allow you to have £100 left over at the end of the month is so believable, so reachable that it prompts its own achievement. Once you believe in the goal, reaching it becomes so very easy.

The figure of £100 is a great place to start, but why stop there? Once you realise the power of this simple sum, you will want to increase the amount, always within your level of comfort and your belief in what is achievable. The first real target is 10 per cent of your income. There are a few simple things you can do with the 10 per cent, which we will look at in later chapters, but for now just concentrate on finding it. Then aim for 20 per cent and even 30 per cent.

SPEND LESS THAN YOU EARN

This is not some fabulous new discovery on my part. This truth has been around from the earliest times. But in recent decades the fuss and clamour of gaudy wealth has become so loud and blinding that this simple, quiet truth cannot be heard above the noise. The ancient Babylonian parables are hailed as the greatest of all inspirational works on the subject of thrift, financial planning and personal wealth. The author George S. Clason brought them to the attention of the world in 1926 in his first edition of *The Richest Man in Babylon*. This timeless book has now been reprinted no fewer than eleven times. He writes: 'Impress yourself with the idea. Fill yourself with the thought. Then take whatever portion seems wise. Let it be not less than one-tenth and lay it by. Arrange your other expenditures to do this if necessary. But lay by that portion first. Soon you will realise what a rich feeling it is to own a treasure upon which you alone have claim. As it grows it will stimulate you. A new joy of life will thrill you.'

I cannot overstate the impact of this simple information. This single act will have more impact on your future finances than any single other action ever. It is simply *spending less than you earn*. You might think that this does not sound sexy or fun, but you can take my word for it: this is where all the fun happens in our financial lives. That dream home, the three-day working week, the retirement in Spain or just not having to work every day to pay bills until the day you drop dead, are all hiding in the difference between what you earn and what you spend. And more than that, that course you want to take, the job change you've always wanted to make, that business you've always wanted to start all live there too.

PAYING FOR TODAY, PROVIDING FOR TOMORROW

Your income has two functions. First, as you know, it has to pay for your current lifestyle. Second, it ought to contribute to setting up your future. If you use all your income to pay for now then you have none left over to put towards tomorrow. That is exactly what we are encouraged to do with our money. Even worse, as our national newspapers remind us every day, a large percentage of the population use all their income plus some they borrow from the future in the form of credit cards, loans and leasing agreements to pay for now.

It wouldn't be so bad if we were all totally happy and fulfilled spending all our income now. But we're not. It may be what everyone does, but it doesn't work. I'm not suggesting you stop going out and save all your money for zimmer frames. I am suggesting that you take your monthly income and *before* you do anything else, you put £100 or 10 per cent towards tomorrow. It's easier than it sounds. How many times have you set up direct debits for something and then just paid them month after month forgetting that you even had them. This time, you would be paying yourself. What a bonus.

This simple, easily accessible, easily achievable wealth-building strategy, also known as the principle of 'paying yourself first' will change for ever the way you feel about money. But before you can decide on whether or not you will put 10 per cent towards tomorrow, you have to know what that 10 per cent is. You already know your income and your expenditure. The exercises in this chapter will help you identify your own personal 10 per cent.

A new joy of life will thrill you

'A new joy of life will thrill you.' Could that be possible? Could it be that simple? Could such an achievable amount of money, such an accessible monetary figure actually hold the feeling not just of contentment or absence of stress, but 'a new joy of life'? The risk: reward ratio in this scenario has always seemed to me to be worth a try.

Let's recap. Here are two approaches to wealth-building.

Approach 1

Work hard for years (or win the lottery) and hope to earn hundreds of thousands, perhaps even millions, hoping that you might be one of the wealthy who become happier even though statistically it has been proven that many won't be happier and most will be unhappier.

Approach 2

Rearrange your finances slightly so you save just 10 per cent of what you earn, do it this month and begin immediately to be filled with a new joy of life.

Since most have tried approach one and are finding it tough going, I am sure I don't need to point out the advantages of giving this second approach a try. The effort you need to put in is less, you will find out much faster if it is working or not, and you won't have to wait nervously until retirement. You don't even need to risk your important relationships or health in the process. Since this message was spoken in Babylonian times, it has been repeated by many great people. But since it's not about loud success or flashy achievement, it has been drowned out. It's as if we are running so fast to keep up with approach number one we have missed the simplicity of approach number two. The tortoise and the hare come to mind. I don't know about you, but I got tired of being the hare; the tortoise gets to enjoy the journey and still win the race. Now that's what I call a good deal.

THE WORK

1. Calculate your monthly net profit/loss. You already know your monthly income figure and your monthly expenses figure. Subtract your expenses from your income. What is the figure?

- If the result is a positive figure, that is if your income is higher than your expenses, you have a monthly net profit. This is the amount you keep every month
- If the result is a negative figure, that is if your income is lower than your expenses, then you have a monthly net loss

2. Create or improve your net income figure. Look at your NTH list from Chapter 3 and go through the items one by one.

- Mark the things you are paying for that no longer give you any pleasure or enough pleasure to make them worthwhile spending your hard-earned cash on
- Mark items that you feel guilty paying for (such as a gym membership you never use)
- Ask yourself on each item, 'Is this item (or a percentage of this item) worth more than my future financial security?'
- When you have examined how you feel about each NTH, make a list of the items you want to dump
- Add up the amount of money you will save by doing this. Congratulations, you have just improved your net income by this amount *every* month

3. Make a fresh start. Open a new bank account into which you will put £100 per month from next month onwards. Open it with £1 if you have to. Even if you have no idea where the £100 will come from, commit to yourself that you will do this one thing for your financial future. Do not concern yourself with what you will do with this money for now. Just give yourself the message that you are serious about keeping at least £100 from now on.

4. Value what you keep. Take a walk through your home and really look around you. How much of what you possess do you truly value? How much of what you have do you still enjoy? Stand in front of a picture and ask yourself if you feel pleasure. You know what I'm talking about. We all have a few things in our lives that consistently, repeatedly give us a warm glow. This is how your possessions make you feel when they are savoured and valued rather than rabidly consumed. Make a list of the things you own that enrich your senses and your life. Add to the list when you think of other things that you don't yet have that would do the same. At the same time begin to dispose of items you possess that don't make you feel fabulous.

5. Reward yourself. I think it's time for a reward. You've come so far. Take £100 and see what you can do with it. Spend it, put it in your new savings account, put it towards a debt, give it to charity. Whatever works for you, just get in touch with the feeling of what it would be like to have £100 left over at the end of every month to do what you like with. Write a paragraph about how that feels.

Key idea

When it comes to happiness, a little money goes a long way.

6

Know How Much You Owe

Too many of us are spending money we haven't earned, to buy things we don't need, to impress people we don't like

ANONYMOUS

Debt has become one of the hottest subjects of our generation for all the wrong reasons. Think back to the headlines of the young father who committed suicide over the shame of his escalating debt or the elderly grandmother who found herself hauled into court when her original £5,000 loan turned into £40,000+. Few things fuel our emotions like the injustice of lives ruined over money. Why is it that no one is ashamed or afraid to apply for credit, or that the credit companies are not ashamed or afraid to advertise credit? But when credit becomes debt, shame and fear close in, keeping people in serious trouble from asking for help, pushing individuals to the brink of what their nerves can handle and sometimes over.

Let's take some of the heat out of this emotional subject before we start. Not all debt is bad debt. The credit industry was born of a need to lend money to people to do great things they might not otherwise be able to do. I like 'good' debt. It gives me the ability to take advantage of opportunities I might not otherwise be able to grasp, such as investing in property. I don't like 'bad' debt: borrowing money to buy something today that will not be worth more tomorrow, such as cars, holidays or groceries. There's no point in being indignant about how unfair the credit industry is. I am happy that measures are being taken to hold the credit industry to account for its activities. Things will get better in due course and you will see less of the kind of easy, high-interest, high-penalty, cruel credit that has pervaded in recent years. But if we demand that the government must regulate the credit industry, surely we must also demand some degree of self-regulation too. When advertisements land on your doormat promising easy credit for all sorts of purchases that would not help you to build wealth, you have a choice. You can just say, 'No.'

SAY NO TO DEBT

There is tremendous collective power in individual restraint. Spurred on by the success of their credit card in the UK, Egg, the one-time on-line banking company, decided to duplicate their strategy in France. They repeated their simple but very effective UK approach of launching huge, tantalising, direct-marketing campaigns. You know the kind of colourful, expertly designed leaflets telling you about the holiday you could have instantly, or the new car you could drive away today just by calling the number now and accepting the pre-approved amount with few questions asked. Less than twelve months after the launch, Egg were forced to pay millions to extricate themselves from France. It turned out the French did not have a taste for borrowing. Using credit to pay for luxuries did not make sense to them. They looked at the glossy leaflets and just said, '*Non.*' It can be that easy. Meanwhile, however, many are living with the consequences of having said, 'Yes, please!' You can't change what has happened in the past, but you can get smart about what you can do from here. So let's move on.

Most people think that getting out of debt is about money. Most people think that if only they could get a big windfall all would be solved. This is rarely the case. The habits that got you into debt will not change just because you suddenly get some extra money. But I hear you say, 'If I owe £6,934.25 and I find £7,000 on the street, hey presto, I'm out of debt.' Sure you are, for the moment. But let's look at what else is going on. How many times have you got a little windfall? Or have you sold an asset or even re-mortgaged or re-consolidated your loans to give you that cash injection that would get you out of debt? Did it work? Why not? What else solves debt problems other than money?

> Money might get you out of debt but honesty will keep you there

Let's be honest. I mean that literally. Being really, really honest is key to healthy finances, especially if you want to be debt-free. Having more money might *get* you of debt, but it will not *keep* you out of debt. Honesty with yourself and others is what will keep you out of debt long term. There are many ways to be financially dishonest. Spending more than you can afford so you can look more successful than you are is a major one. Remember what we said about appearances in Chapter 2? This is where keeping up those appearances gets funded from. What about overstating your earnings to financial institutions so that you will get more credit than you would otherwise be eligible for, or 'forgetting' to declare some commitments?

I know these things. I see them all the time in client files. No one means to be dishonest, it just happens in the way we 'arrange' things in our heads. We compartmentalise all the pieces of the jigsaw and that allows us to go on not having to tell the whole clear truth to anyone, least of all to ourselves. I can tell very quickly if a client is serious about dealing with their debt by their willingness (or otherwise) to take one simple action. That is telling someone close to them about the reality of their financial situation. When this happens, they have broken the spell that debt has over them and they are free. You see, there is the debt. Then there is the secret of the debt. Carrying the debt is one thing, but carrying the secret of debt is actually the heavier load. I understand you don't want to tell the world everything about your personal money. That's common sense. That's why it is important to understand the subtle difference between healthy financial self-containment and unhealthy financial secrecy.

KEEP YOUR OWN COUNSEL

I encourage healthy financial self-containment. This is the kind of steady self-confidence with your financial situation that allows you to sit quietly with your own circumstances. It's where you are comfortable with your money situation, even if you are dealing with debt, *especially* if you are dealing with debt. If you do need help or information with a specific area, you decide who can best inform you, you get the help, you apply it and get on with your business in the same quiet manner. Unhealthy financial secrecy, on the other hand, is where you are in a difficult situation and neither speak of it, nor ask for help even as the situation only gets worse.

Rather than being the quiet of confidence, it is the quiet that hides humiliation, guilt and fear.

I want you to commit to yourself that you will not live a lie. Commit to honesty from here on. Just because you have not handled money well to date does not make you a bad person, a failure or any of the things you may feel being in debt means. It just means that you made some mistakes. Now you have asked for help and are learning how to do better. That is something to be proud of.

I believe that a client who comes to me wanting to get rid of their debt has both the possibility and the capability to be completely in charge of themselves and their money. I believe that when they have the information, skills and tools they need to make informed decisions about their actions and the consequences of those actions, they will choose wisely. This is why you won't find me asking you to go through the emotional drama of cutting up your credit cards. By asking you to cut up your credit cards, I would give you two messages. First, that you are a helpless victim, powerless to withstand the external forces stacked against you. Second, that you do not have the intelligence or courage to be in command of yourself and your actions. I simply do not accept either of those two things about any of my clients.

Being in debt does not make you a failure or a bad person

Let's both be honest with each other. We both know that the debt you have accrued over a long period of time may take a little while to repay. It may not take as long as you think when you apply the techniques we will discuss later, but nor is it going to disappear overnight. What if there was a way that you could have the debt, but lose the fear, guilt and shame that create the need for such secrecy? Wouldn't that help in the meantime? What if I told you that you don't have to wait to be out of debt to be free of the pressures of debt? What if I told you that you could have a sense of financial ease even with the debt you have?

MAKE YOUR OWN REPAYMENT PLAN

The key is to replace the repayment plan drawn up by the lender with your own repayment plan. The main reason why debt is so uncomfortable is because the plan laid out for you by the credit institution is their plan for their benefit. There are two basic elements of debt. First there is the original amount that you agreed to borrow. Then there is the interest payment that gets added either at the beginning (for example fixed-rate loans or HP agreements), or which accrues as you go along (such as with credit cards and store cards). The credit company's plan for your debt is to add as much interest as possible to the original amount borrowed. When you replace their plan with your plan, you put yourself in charge of your debt. You choose how much interest you will pay and when. You choose clarity and power over fear and shame. You win.

THE FIVE-POINT PLAN FOR STRESS-FREE DEBT

1. Identify exactly how much and to whom you owe money (list your debts according to the instructions below).
2. Know exactly what resources you have to apply to the debt (start with the magic £100 you found in the last chapter).
3. Re-apply the resources in the optimal manner possible to eliminate your debt in the shortest possible time (select one debt towards which you will pay the extra £100).
4. Set up the structures, direct debits etc., to put your new plan into action.
5. Resurrect your dreams and goals so you can get on with achieving them (now you know your debt is being taken care of).

IDENTIFY AND PRIORITISE YOUR DEBT

The first thing to do is to stop adding to your debt by spending less than you earn. Next, if you have only fixed-rate loans, choose the debt with the shortest time left to pay. If you have credit card debt, choose the debt with the highest interest rate. If you have more than one with the same interest rate, pick the one with the shortest time left to pay. If you have difficulty calculating the timeline on a credit card repayment schedule (and who doesn't) from those with the highest rates, pick the card with the smallest amount. What is the minimum monthly payment you have to make per month to the debt you have selected? Divide the total amount of the debt by the minimum monthly payment. Note how many months will it take to pay it off using this calculation. Get a calendar and plot what date that will be. Now, add £100 to the minimum payment. Divide the total owed by that new amount. How many months is that? What date will that now be? Isn't there an amazing difference? When applied to fixed-rate loans this technique will significantly reduce the duration of the debt. When applied to credit card debt this technique will totally shrivel both the duration of the debt and the amount you pay in interest.

CLAIRE'S STORY

Claire had mixed fixed-loan and credit card debt. Her first selected credit card had a debt of £5,000, with a monthly minimum payment of 5 per cent of the outstanding balance, currently £250. Using the credit company's payment structure it would take over fifteen and a half years to pay the debt. Paying just an additional £100 per month cut that time to less than two and a half years. Would spending £100 less per month on little extras have a dramatic impact on your lifestyle? I doubt it. But it makes a life-changing difference to the length of time it will take you to become debt-free.

Why is £100 so powerful? It's because it can turn the tide of interest working against you. Take again the real-life example of Claire. Her minimum monthly payment of £250 was allocated with £72.50 going towards interest and only £177.50 going towards reducing the debt. When she added £100 to the minimum payment of £250, and paid £350, then the amount paid in interest in that month was still £72.50 but £277.50 came off the total debt owed. Now things were moving in her favour. All she did was keep making the repayments she already had on all other debts and put an extra £100 towards one at a time. Are you excited yet?

It gets even better. You have seen what can happen when you put £100 towards one of your debts. When you have finished paying off the first debt you select the next one according to the same criteria. This time, you add together the next minimum monthly payment plus the amount you were paying towards the first debt (the minimum monthly payment of the old debt + the extra £100) and pay that amount to the second debt.

For Claire, that meant that she took £350 that she

was paying towards the first debt and put it towards the next debt which was another credit card debt of £4,000. The original monthly minimum payment on this second card was £95, which would have taken over sixty-one years to pay off. By now paying £445 (£95 + £350) that time was cut to within ten months. From sixty-one years to ten months. Are you excited now?

KEEP GOING

And so on, and so on. Every time you pay off a debt, you add the money you were paying to that debt to the minimum payment of the next debt and pay that amount. As time goes past, your payments get larger and larger and interest working against you has less and less chance to be significant. Result: you get out of debt in a shorter time than you originally would have, pay much less interest than you otherwise would have and all at a true short-term cost to your lifestyle of £100 per month.

That's the basic principle. You are a smart person. If you can do this on £100, imagine what you could do with £200. Be careful about making the plan too tight. You want to have enough money to enjoy your life while you pay off your debt. There is no surer way to get fed up and give up on the plan than to attempt to put your current life on hold while you pay for the past. It has taken years to accumulate your debt, so allow yourself a few years to get out of it too.

> It has taken years to accumulate your debt, so allow your-
> self a few years to get out of it too

COMMUNICATION IS KEY

No matter how bad the situation is, communicate with
your creditors. Set up your plan your way and call them
and inform them what you are planning to do. Most
creditors will be glad to hear from you and, when
approached with integrity and dignity on your part, are
supportive. When choosing which debts to pay first, as
well as calculating those with the highest rates, pay
attention to those that bug you the most. Often if you
borrow from friends or family there is no interest rate.
But seeing the person every day and knowing you owe
money can sometimes be uncomfortable. If you are
uncomfortable about a private debt, consider paying it
off as a priority. Remember, the important thing is to
have debt without the negative emotions.

Consider any legal consequences of your debt. Some
debts carry specific penalties, which can be serious. For
example monies owed to the Inland Revenue automatically carry legal and monetary penalties, but money owed
to your Auntie Joan will not. If you have serious debt and
you have any doubt, get help. Contact your local Citizens
Advice Bureau and find out what you need to know.

REWARD YOURSELF

Plan to reward yourself along the way for significant milestones. Every time you pay a debt in full take a payment holiday and spend the magic £100 on yourself. If the first debt takes longer than a year to pay, take a portion of the £100 twice yearly and treat yourself. Plan it now. What will you do, where will you go? How are you going to make it special and relevant to your achievement and honour yourself?

Sometimes on a journey you can get a little off track. As soon as you realise you are off the plan, go back to the map (calculator and repayment schedule), plot where you are now and begin again. Watch out for Christmas, holidays, birthdays and other big events. Watch out for when the washing machine gets broken and needs to be fixed. Look ahead and see if there are possible challenges to your plan looming and prepare for them as much as you can. Debt need not cripple you. It can if you let it, but you can make your own plan and repay even large debts and still have a life.

Lose the money, don't lose the lesson

When I look out into our society and see the enormous debt amassed, I don't see a hopeless economic situation as many are purporting. I see a nation with the opportunity to be the greatest wealth-builders for generations. Being in debt and getting out of it is one of the best financial training courses available. People who have been in debt and have learned how to get out of it have had to learn valuable skills that are fundamental to subsequent wealth-building. They learn to understand themselves, to be in command of their emotions and to trust their own judgement. They learn to replace fear, guilt and worry with trust, courage and commitment. They learn to live within their means. They learn a keen eye for prices. They learn how interest works and the power of being on the right side of it. They learn to be happy with whatever they have or don't have and that is the most important lesson of all. You have paid a high price for these lessons, but you have received the best possible financial training there is and that is priceless.

THE WORK

1. Face the facts. First you need to know what you are dealing with. Go back to the list of liabilities you made when you calculated your net worth in Chapter 2.

	Liabilities (everything you OWE)	Amount	Interest Rate	Mthly Pymt	Months to pay off/Date	Repayment Agreement	Contact details
M	**Accounts Payable** (outstanding bills such as electricity or telephone, which you have used but not yet paid.)						
N	**Business Loan** (any monies you have been loaned to put into a business)						
O	**Credit cards** (write the total amount you owe on each credit card)						
P	**Lines of credit** (this includes hire purchase or lease agreements such as for your car and shop credit such as store cards)						
Q	**Personal debts** (monies owed to friends and family)						
R	**Mortgages on investment properties**						
S	**Mortgage** on your principal, private residence						
T	**Total Liabilities (add lines M–S)** (the value of everything you OWE if you had to pay it all today)						

This time note the interest rate and monthly payment for each item. Calculate the timeline for each. Write the name and contact details of each person or institution alongside the specific title of the debt. In particular with private debt (debt borrowed from friends or family), write the specific details of the arrangement you have to pay them back. If you don't have an arrangement, agree one. Put all the information you have about each debt here in one place.

2. Tell someone about your debt. Choose someone to whom you will talk about your real financial situation in the next twenty-four hours: a friend or a professional. Call the Citizens Advice Bureau, call a financial coach, get someone on your side. Debt is one of those problems that is truly halved when shared.

3. Pick your first debt, apply £100. Select your first debt according to the criteria above and apply £100 extra payment per month. Set up the payment by direct debit towards that debt and note in your diary when you need to review the plan and move on to the next debt.

4. Lose the money, don't lose the lesson. What have you learned from being in debt that will serve you now as you move from debt to prosperity? What lessons have you learned that you can use to build wealth successfully and to pass on to the younger people in your life so that they do not suffer from the same mistakes? Write the answers in your notebook.

5. Begin to visualise your debt-free life. Begin now to visualise your debt-free life. What will that look like for you? What will you be able to be, do and have and what will you be able to do for others? Add up the total monthly debt repayments you are currently paying plus £100. That is the amount of money you will have per month to do as you wish with, once your debt is paid off. Dream a little.

Key idea

The debt is yours, make the repayment plan your own too.

7

Know Where You Are Starting From

Money, it turned out, was exactly like sex,
you thought of nothing else if you didn't have it
and thought of other things if you did

JAMES BALDWIN

A young tourist, lost on a country road in Ireland, was looking for directions when he spotted an old man leaning on a gate. 'Can you tell me how to get to Dublin?' he enquired. The old man took a thoughtful breath and replied, 'Well now, if I was you, I wouldn't start from here.' It's an old joke that always gets a laugh. After all, it's absurd to suggest someone could start from anywhere other than where they are. And yet, how often have you heard or perhaps even said, 'I'll start that diet on Monday,' or 'When I get that new job, I'll put some money aside,' or 'When I win the lottery, I'll give money to charity'? In other words, 'When I am somewhere else, I'll start out in the direction I really want to go.'

Instead of looking longingly into the distance wishing you were somewhere else, just focus on where you are now. This is where you are starting from. However much money you have or don't have, however much money you earn or don't earn, however much money you owe or have saved, only when you know exactly where you are can you begin to plan how to get to where you want to be. It's like one of those town maps you see at train stations. No matter where you want to go to, the first thing you have to find is the big red arrow that says 'You Are Here'. Once you know your position, you can take note of the major landmarks between where you are and where you want to be. Then it's just a matter of focusing on one landmark after another until you arrive.

AUTOMATIC WEALTH

The reason why knowing this simple information can transform your life is because, once laid, a good financial plan runs on autopilot. As soon as you know clearly where you are, your first personal financial landmark will become clear to you. When you programme the autopilot to reach that landmark, you can forget all about it until you get there. For example, your first landmark might be to put aside £1,000 this year. You've done your 'Find the smile' exercise from Chapter 3 and decided that you could do without the full gym membership you rarely use. It happens to be £1,000 per year. The key is that at the same time as you cancel your order to pay the gym, you also set up a new direct debit for the same amount from your current account to the new savings account you opened in Chapter 5. Lo and behold, in one year's time, you will have 'automatically' reached your first financial landmark. It's the same with any financial goal. If your first goal is to pay off one selected debt, set up a standing order for the monthly payment plus the 'magic £100' and forget about it. Programme the autopilot, get on with your life and let your money work for itself.

While it might seem that you need to spend an inordinate amount of time looking into your personal money situation over the course of these exercises, take heart. It is only while you learn to understand your financial situation that you will need to give this level of attention to money. It's a one-off investment of your time. Once you have gathered your basic financial information and decided on your first personal financial goal, you can afford to think less about money. When you reach your first financial goal, you will need to invest a little time again to set up the next goal and off you go again. It is a common misconception that those with money are obsessed with money and think of nothing else. The opposite is more likely to be true.

> When you put your money on auto-pilot, you're free to look out the window and dream

Whatever financial starting point you are at, your journey will be greatly enhanced if you leave behind negative financial emotion: fear, guilt, frustration, sadness, envy and so on. This journey you are taking may seem to be a journey about money, but it is invariably a journey of personal and emotional growth. Fear is the primary negative emotion that accompanies money problems. It's also the most dangerous emotion to attach to money because fear blocks good decision-making. It is also the easiest to eliminate. Knowledge cuts through fear like a light cuts through the dark: knowing your basic numbers, knowing how much you earn, knowing how much you spend, knowing how much you owe, knowing how much you repay towards debt and for how long, knowing how much you have to keep. These simple facts smash through the powerlessness that keeps you in cyclical, debilitating fear.

LEAVE THE PAST BEHIND YOU

Don't worry about what has gone before. Let the past belong to the past. Whatever financial mistakes you have made, there is always a way out. I have seen some truly desperate financial situations turned around. As a stock market trader, I have watched ordinary people gamble all their savings, borrow as much as they could get their hands on, re-mortgage their homes and sell other solid investments to chase the get-rich-quick fix of the markets only to lose everything. Many never trade again, some do the same thing over again, sometimes many times. A few get up, dust themselves down and begin to approach the market, themselves and their money with a new respect. Then I know they have begun the journey for real. As a financial coach I have seen fearful clients with enormous debts and little income make their way to prosperity, and unhappy clients with large incomes put the balance back into their lives. In the end they all have one thing in common: money is the least of their motivations. Those who pursue a more mature understanding of their attitude to money and are managing their finances quietly, steadily and successfully are some of the most balanced, happy and generous people I have the pleasure to know. Mostly you would not even guess they ever had money problems, nor would you guess they are now as wealthy as they are. Living full and happy lives is their priority.

I don't have an amazing, against-the-odds, rags-to-riches story to impress you with or to prove my case. I'm not one of those people who went from crippling debt to a £1 million business and can show you how to do the same. I'm an ordinary woman who realised that the process I was taught (or was neglected to be taught) to build my financial life on had major flaws and set out to find a better way. If I had been taught simple truths about money properly in my teens or earlier, I would have had a much more rewarding and easier financial journey. Truths like 'spend less than you earn', 'pay yourself first', the difference between good debt and bad debt, the importance of valuing what you own and owning only what you value and, the great granddaddy of them all, the sheer importance of the emotion you attach to money. I would have had more room for laughter and spent less time chasing a living.

> Happiness is the main attraction, financial success is just a sideshow

If I had known years ago what I know now, I could have saved myself years of believing that money held the key to security and freedom, the freedom to step off the rat race, work at what makes me happy and simply enjoy living my life. More importantly, I could have saved myself years of believing that somehow being financially successful would bring me that most elusive thing of all, contentment. Quite simply, I would have realised that contentment comes first; it is just there for the taking and when you take it, money follows.

I'm not against material wealth but nor do I want to

move to the country and keep my own chickens. I enjoy my possessions and all the great experiences money can buy and I also enjoy the simpler things in life like having time to take a walk in the woods. Somewhere in between the 'good-lifers' who make the headlines by swapping a Ferrari in the City for a tractor on the farm (or disappear from any kind of decent life) and those celeb millionaires who make the remainder of the headlines are the rest of us. And there are many, many more of us than there are of all of them put together. So why do we live our lives hankering after either extreme? Especially when a fabulous ordinary life is so easily achievable and so deeply rewarding. Why take the wild-goose chase that is the constant pursuit of wealth? Take the time to amass non-financial assets; such as good health, being home with the kids instead of burning the midnight oil, putting your knowledge and love into your family instead of all your energy into your bank account. You will leave their hearts full of love and that is currency that will carry them further than just money. Set up your finances to progress automatically and set yourself free to go out into the world in pursuit of your dreams alone. Now that would really be fun. That is your reward for taking these simple actions of personal financial management.

FOLLOW YOUR OWN PATH

The challenge of our time is not getting what you want, but knowing what you don't want. We have so much choice; we can 'have it all'. But even if you really had enough money to 'have it all' there just is not time enough in one life, even a long life, to do everything, see everything and have everything. It is just not possible. Therefore the choice we need to make is the choice of what *not* to do and what *not* to have. But it is a choice we are ill equipped for. The sheer abundance and relative affordability of material possessions have multiplied exponentially in recent decades and rather than being delighted at the extended choices available to us, as our predecessors were, we consume all we can and relish little.

THE FIRST LEVEL

There are two main stages to becoming financially balanced. Some people are happy to get to the first stage, others move on to the second stage and a very few people add a third of their own design. Not all stages are for everyone, not because they cannot achieve them, but because they may choose not to. They may choose to direct their energies to alternative pursuits according to their own talents and gifts, and the world is a richer place for that. The first level is for everyone. It is a place of contentment and security with money, a place that allows you to live your life fully today, provide adequately for your future and to give a little to those less fortunate. It's a place where you institute the simple fundamentals of money management that will position you in that lovely 10 per cent band of most contribution to your happiness, and everyone deserves that. These financial fundamentals include all the things we have already talked about such as spending less than you earn and some we'll touch on in this chapter such as setting up your own personal emergency fund and making some provision for your future.

If you do nothing else after this book, putting these fundamentals in place will bring you a financial foundation of stability and security. It's the financial equivalent of brushing your teeth. I bet you barely notice yourself brushing your teeth in the morning and the evening every day of your life since you were little. And yet if you had not done so, you would be living with terrible pain and trauma over simple things like eating. Brushing your teeth is that trivial and that important. So are the basics of money management. Just take regular care of your money according to the easy, simple exercises detailed in this book and you will give yourself a beautiful smile and the ability to taste the best of life. Where you go from there is up to you. We have already talked about most of the elements so let's finish off with the remainder.

SET UP AN EMERGENCY FUND

An emergency fund is just that, a fund you keep for emergencies. Very often we go along on a monthly basis paying our bills and keeping ahead (just) until something happens. You might have to take sick leave from or lose your job (or choose to change a job), which means the family has a short period of reduced or inconsistent income. This can put unnecessary additional pressure on an already pressured situation. A real practical step towards financial security is to have a little cash put aside. How much should that be? Action item 1 will help you calculate your personal target amount. With even just a little bit of money in the bank you will begin to know what it feels like to be rich. Be careful, it's contagious, you'll want to feel more of it. You might even get to enjoy putting money aside.

Finally, it is important to have adequate insurance and pension provision. Make sure you have made provision for both according to your own comfort level. Until you are in a position to understand and provide for your own financial future to the level you would ideally like, choose one of the methods and products available currently. Get a good independent financial adviser who can help you decide what is right for you and protect and provide for your future.

RECLAIM YOUR DREAMS

When you put your personal finances in order your whole life changes. Particularly when you spend 10 per cent less than you earn, you don't just free up the money, you get the priceless freedom in your head, to think, to dream, to plan, to allow for creativity, fun, enjoyment and time for you, free from money worries, stress and pressure. This is the kind of mental environment that supports great ideas, great solutions to the problems of your life and of the world. I firmly believe that the energy that could be used to fulfil your dreams or which could be applied to solve many of the world's problems is being wasted every day in cyclical destructive thinking patterns that leave you tired and weary, patterns mostly about money. If your life is short on financial security and you live in financial stress, there is little room for solutions or possibilities, neither for your own life nor others.

I know you are not someone who is reading this book so you can make lots of money to hoard away selfishly. I know you are a person who wants to address your financial challenges so you can get on with the things that move you. First, what are the things that you would really like to do? Perhaps you have always wanted to trek in the Himalaya or go to a Milan fashion show, run a marathon or take a year off to sail around the world or to stay at home with your children. That done, as a fulfilled individual, what would you do to improve your community, your country or the world? What problem in your community or the world would you like to address? Who or what would you take care of, if everything in your life were taken care of?

In 2002, at the height of the dot com boom, a young father of two sold his enormously successful, US-based, IT company for $488 million. Having started from a garage with nothing, this was the kind of pay day that many dream of. There was nothing unusual about what he had done; the late 1990s gave the world many IT millionaires. But Phillip Berber, a young man from Dublin, and his wife Donna, from the East End of London, were different. They were a couple who knew how much they earned, how much they spent and, most significantly, how much they needed to keep. So they knew they could give away $100 million and did just that. Phillip Berber also quit all commercial activities, decided which of the world's problems he could make a difference to and now works exclusively as a 'social entrepreneur', bringing his skills and experience as a successful businessman to the business of making the world a better place.

THE POWER OF ORDINARY MONEY

He is not alone. There is a noticeable movement of people who are financially secure who are making 'social investment' a modern phenomenon. Take Bob Geldof who pioneered the concept with Live Aid, and Bono who works tirelessly for the elimination of Third World debt. But just as you don't have to be a celeb millionaire to be happy, nor do you have to wait to have millions of pounds to make an impact on the world. Twenty-five pounds will support a Romanian orphan for a month, £2 will build a well for a village in Honduras, £1 will provide literacy for thirty children in Burma, a few pence will save a bear or a dolphin. 'During the last three decades a money revolution has transformed personal finance,' says *Business Week Online* in an article in September 2001 reporting on the 'democratization of finance'. Imagine if every family in the UK (21.6 million according to the 2001 census), were to give £20 per month towards combating world poverty. It's a level of investment that is within the reach of most. Just £20 per household per month from 20 million families in the UK, would amount to £4.8 *billion* pounds in a year. And that would be *every* year; a small individual amount but the impact would be something that one fabulously wealthy person alone could never sustain. That's enough to care for every Romanian orphan, with enough left over to provide literally countless wells, tools and seeds to Ethiopians to feed themselves and educate thousands of Burmese children. Imagine what that would do to reduce world hunger and poverty. That's the power of ordinary wealth. That's the power you hold.

Congratulations on getting to this final chapter. If you have followed the exercises you will find that it is

easier than you ever thought possible to be happy financially. It is easier than you ever thought to be financially
secure. It is easier than you ever thought to stop
dreaming of the millions you think will make you happy
and start working from where you are, quietly and
steadily. The exercises in this book are not the stuff of
flash gimmicks that feed into the quick-fix and rat-race
ethos. They are simple timeless truths, proven over
aeons. Take a little time to establish a new financial
reality for yourself; the first year makes a huge difference, two turns it all around, then wealth is unavoid-
able. This is where you start from. Stop chasing a lifestyle
and embrace your life. Enjoy your journey. I wish you
well.

THE WORK

1. **Set up an emergency fund.** Calculate how much you
want to put aside and a date by which you will achieve
it. To do this, you must ask yourself if your income were
to cease tomorrow and you had to survive until you found
a new source of income, how long would you like to give
yourself to do that. A rule of thumb is two to twenty-four
months, depending on your own comfort level. Multiply
the number of months you choose by your Must Have
total from Chapter 3. Put two big fat red lines under this
figure. After payment of debt, this is your next goal to
achieve using your £100 or 10 per cent. Divide the total

by the amount that is your monthly net profit and you will find out how many months it is going to take you to fill your emergency fund. Mark this date in your calendar.

2. Count your assets again. Make a list of your most valuable non-financial assets: health, family, friends, free country, the food in your fridge, a roof over your head, the money to buy this book, the fact you can read it. Read it at night before going to sleep; cultivate gratitude – it will carry you far.

3. Dream a little dream for you. Sit quietly and decide what of all the millions of things that you could be, do and have do you really want to be, do and have? Who are you at the heart of you and what is the finest expression of that person? There is nothing that you truly wish to be that you do not have the possibility to express. When you have put your financial house in order, what will you be free to become?

4. Give back. If you don't already have one, add a line to your expense list called 'Tithing' and choose a charity or a good cause to which you will regularly make a contribution. It might only be a few pence to begin with that you will drop into buskers' cans or various outstretched hands on your way to work during the month. There is no better way to remind yourself that no matter how little you have, there are always those who have less and to whom your little will make a big difference. Allow yourself to feel really good about doing this.

5. Celebrate good times. Throw a party. Go to a party. Stay in and have a private party. Whatever you do make sure it has the word 'party' in it. It is important to mark and remember the times you did some things for your benefit. Heaven knows we all remember the bad times easily enough. Do something that will help you remember this time you committed to put a financial plan in place from which you can start to build the life you really want to live.

Key idea

When you stand on a stable platform, you can reach for the stars.

Transform your life
with Hodder Mobius

For the latest information on the best in
Spirituality, Self-Help,
Health & Wellbeing and Parenting,

visit our website
www.hoddermobius.com